WILLIAM BARCLAY:
The Plain Uncommon Man

William Barclay:
The Plain Uncommon Man

Edited by R. D. Kernohan

HODDER AND STOUGHTON
LONDON SYDNEY AUCKLAND TORONTO

British Library Cataloguing in Publication Data

Kernohan, R. D., Ed.
  William Barclay: the plain uncommon man.
  1. Barclay, William
  2. New Testament scholars – Scotland – Biography
  3. Church of Scotland – Biography
  I. Kernohan, R D
  285'.2'0924   BS2351.B28

ISBN 0 340 25381 9

Two appropriate thoughts,
in lieu of dedication

In all my memories of you I have cause for nothing but
thanksgiving . . .

Don't worry about anything. In every circumstance of
life tell God about the things you want to ask him for in
your prayers and your requests to him, and bring him
your thanks too. And God's peace, which is beyond both
our understanding and our contriving, will stand guard
over your hearts and minds, because your life is linked
for ever with the life of Christ Jesus.

*From Paul's Letter to "all God's consecrated people in
Philippi" in William Barclay's translation of the New
Testament, published by Collins.*

The editor of this book, Robert Kernohan, who also wrote the introductory and concluding chapters, is editor of the Church of Scotland's magazine *Life and Work*, in which much of William Barclay's writing appeared. He is a journalist (and Church elder) who was formerly London Editor of the *Glasgow Herald* and has also worked in politics, serving a term as the Conservative Party's Scottish Director. At Glasgow University and Balliol College, Oxford, he was a historian, not a theologian, and he is the author of a book on Scottish history as seen through Church journalism.

Details of the other contributors to the book appear before their individual contributions.

Acknowledgments

I am grateful to many people who have made this book possible, and not least to the Publications Committee of the
Church of Scotland and the Saint Andrew Press for their
co-operation. I am also grateful to the contributors. They are
not responsible for each other's opinions, nor for mine. I do
not necessarily agree with all they have written, except in so
far as I think all the opinions deserve to be heard and read.

Others who deserve individual thanks are Mr Ronald
Barclay for his help and understanding when the possibility of
this book first arose (though no opinion in it is in any way
attributable to him) and Miss Ellen McGillivray for under-
taking my typing.

The pieces used as examples of William Barclay's technique
first appeared in the Church of Scotland's monthly *Life and
Work* and I would thank the editor for his gracious permission
to use them, were I not myself the editor. Two of them later
appeared in book form published by the Saint Andrew Press.
The quotations from Barclay's New Testament are from his
definitive translation, published by Collins, and not from the
working version interspersed with commentary in the *Daily
Study Bible*, published by the Saint Andrew Press, from which
I have occasionally quoted comments by Barclay.

The chapter on Barclay as broadcaster first appeared in the
autobiography of Ronald Falconer posthumously published
by the Handsel Press, Edinburgh, as *The Kilt beneath my
Cassock*. I am grateful for permission to include it here.

Although I myself have not quoted from the book (except
for the occasional phrase which matched opinions which
Barclay expressed at various times and places) I add my special
debt to his *Testament of Faith*, published by Mowbrays. This
simple book provides confirmation of his belief and attitudes
in compact form and also, by his own testimony, explodes
some myths about him. Clearly, it also impressed others who
admired him, close at hand or from afar.

But Barclay's views, thoughts, life, and work are scattered over so many books and much other writing that it is hard to cite them all. I, and the readers, ought to acknowledge most to him.

EDINBURGH, CHRISTMAS 1979

Contents

The cover photograph of William Barclay is by John Atkinson.

1 – The man this book is about: William Barclay (1907–1978)

William Barclay, who was author of well over fifty Christian books, was Professor of Divinity and Biblical Criticism at Glasgow University from 1963 to 1974. He was also an outstanding broadcaster, first on radio and later on television. Before going to Glasgow University as a New Testament lecturer in 1946, he had for thirteen years been a parish minister of the Church of Scotland in Renfrew, a Clydeside industrial town on the south-west fringe of Glasgow.

Barclay's parents came from Fort William in the West Highlands but he was born at Wick, near John o'Groats. His father was a bank manager. Willie Barclay, however, really belonged to the Lanarkshire steel town of Motherwell, where the family moved when he was five. He went from the local Dalziel High School to Glasgow University and did post-graduate study at Marburg in Germany. His divinity studies had begun in the Glasgow college of the United Free Church of Scotland just before it united with the other Presbyterian tradition of the "Auld Kirk" to form the Church of Scotland of modern times.

His biggest work was the *Daily Study Bible*, a guidebook to the New Testament for the general reader, which began "almost accidently" with a hastily commissioned study of the Acts of the Apostles. It was first published in the 1950's and has later been revised. Barclay also produced a complete, modern translation of the New Testament and several books of prayers; but most of the books were about the faith and background of New Testament Christianity, and its relevance to life today.

William Barclay died in 1978. He had continued to write till almost the end of his life and had briefly been a Visiting Professor at Strathclyde University, formerly Glasgow's

Royal Technical College. He was survived by his wife (who died in 1979), a son, and a daughter. Another daughter was drowned in a sailing accident. He said that Jesus stilled the storm in his heart provoked by this tragic grief.

To theological liberals Barclay seemed fairly conservative. To many conservative evangelicals he seemed too liberal. He himself thought that the Church needed liberal evangelicals and quoted approvingly Herbert Butterfield's words: "Hold fast to Christ and for the rest be totally uncommitted."

Barclay committed himself with astonishing vigour and skill to many kinds of Christian communication, but he held fast to Christ. What he wrote, did and was, showed him to be a remarkable disciple and apostle of Jesus and one of the great communicators of the twentieth century.

He received D.D. and C.B.E. awards; but far richer honours surely awaited him.

2 – Barclay: apostle of our time
by R. D. Kernohan

I: "In Jesus I see God"

This book is about a very uncommon man who in some ways was a very plain man. Although he was astonishingly success-ful, he was a simple man in some ways, and an unassuming one. He was a good scholar as well as a popular and successful professor; but he was a communicator of genius.

There is a hymn which invites the "gentle Jesus" to pity our simplicity. I love the hymn but am uncertain of its theology. When I think of William Barclay I am more inclined to *envy* his simplicity as well as his talents. The last words I remember hearing from him were of his devotion to Christ, and he could even be, like the earlier apostle and scholar who came from Tarsus, a fool for Christ. For the world would probably account it folly not to fill our barns, our storehouses, and our bank accounts with the last profit we can reap in royalty and fee.

Barclay was a good Christian and a fine scholar but a superb communicator. The goodness which went with his generosity was turned to a kind of greatness in the way he used his scholarship to communicate the good news and high spirits of the Gospel to other Christians. He also reached out to those who wondered if they could be Christians, or were still Christians, or might be Christians after all.

This century has not really been a time for greatness, despite the invocations of the politicians. It is supposed to have been the century of the common man. But the really uncommon men in it have only too often been uncommonly nasty and have given the ordinary plain men and women a terrible time of it.

Barclay put his great talents at the disposal of plain men and women, as their servant — as their minister as well as Christ's. This book is largely an exploration of how he did it and why he was able to do it, as well as a recollection of what he was like while doing it.

In Christian life as well as public life there have been few claims to greatness this century to stand the authentication of passing time and changing fashion.

One can identify great Victorian preachers, even great Victorian prelates, as well as their political contemporaries whom we still think of as great men. In their own day at least, and for a while after, there were also Biblical scholars and theologians, who were acknowledged then as great in influence as well as intellect and scholarship.

It has been far harder to stake such a claim and wield such an influence in this century. It is not a preaching century. It is uncertain, despite the vigour of Biblical scholarship and even more of Biblical translation, to what extent it has remained a Bible-reading century even for the majority of those who call themselves Christian. It is a time when the expansion of education (not always in the West the extension of literacy) has gone with the divorce of scholarship from teaching.

William Barclay went against many of the trends. He was a scholar who extended his role in teaching a few thousand divinity students into teaching millions who read his books and heard his broadcasts. He turned out, fairly late in life, to have a style, character, and personality which were as brilliantly successful on television as his simple, clear style of literary exposition had been in print.

In that (as contributions to this book make clear), he appeared to go against some of the rules as well as the fashions of broadcasting. In fact, he was helped by those who gave scope to his natural talent and personality. He was helped too, as other passages in this book make clear, by his own great powers of application and preparation. But it is important to emphasise that television did not create his exceptional success as a communicator but merely ratified and extended it. He was already the Baedeker of New Testament travel, and had sent many thousands of people into deeper personal exploration past many points of no return.

In editing this book one of the awkward things has been to discover the way in which the Barclay impact on television is still remembered. It was tempting to edit out some of these references to Barclay as a broadcaster. But they are important as evidence of the range of talents that he had and of the kind of personal impact that he also made as a lecturer and in ordinary conversation — in so far as any conversation with him could be called "ordinary". Yet inevitably they are less important now than the gifts of written communication which he had developed before he ever saw the inside of a TV studio and which will keep him for years to come as one of the most important of Christian communicators. Indeed I hope the value of this book will not be mainly to revive affectionate memories but to deepen the interest of those who come to know Barclay as a writer — and who, if they react to their elders as most of us have always done, may be put off rather than attracted by an older generation's enthusiasm for a name, a reputation, and a memory. But I believe that Barclay will retain an appeal across barriers of time just as he has for many years brought help and encouragement across old denominational barriers and (perhaps more significantly) the new demarcation lines created among Christians by divisions which have new names or even, as yet, no names.

Barclay was a Christian who did not wear labels well. It is not easy to fit him into modern categories either in scholarship or in conservative or liberal theological party affiliations. Attempts to fit him into them have often been as uncomfortable as a Procrustean bed, a figure of speech that I feel entitled to use of someone who was so deeply rooted in the classical tradition which local Scottish academies once shared with the English public schools. It now seems to have sadly declined in both.

"I have no politics," he once told me, after something which he had written about education had brought singularly outspoken but not very well informed criticism on both our heads from a peer of the realm. He meant party politics, and I was tempted to tell him that the average Socialist educator's ideas of a comprehensive school — a concept he had defended from the standpoint of Christian ethics — differed in some respects from the Dalziel High School which equipped him to take a First in Classics at Glasgow before he turned to Divinity. But what was true of party politics was also true of theological party lines.

Even now liberals, without much thought and with no malice, find it easy to think of Barclay as conservative in his approach to scholarship, the New Testament, and the Church. But many conservatives found it natural to think of him as a liberal, for example in his approach to such miracles as the stilling of the storm, and some of them denounced him, both for the beliefs he held and for some that he didn't hold at all. It is still possible to find Fundamentalists for whom he was just another university heretic, more dangerous than others because he was more popular. In our time, after all, some of the most destructive heresies have been tempered by their own tedium.

There has been nothing tedious about Barclay, but it is as a believer and encourager of belief, not as a doctrinal adventurer that he should be remembered.

He was what he himself called a "natural believer", never doubting either God or the love of God. He was also, as he made clear himself in his brief autobiography and as his friend James Martin shows again in this book, a believer in the life to come, on which he said the teaching of the New Testament was based. Indeed where he himself agreed he might go beyond "strict orthodoxy" was in believing that ultimately all humanity will be gathered into the love of God, relying on Biblically based arguments from the Gospels and Epistles as well as the nature of the God revealed in Jesus. "In Jesus," he said, "I see God." Moreover he believed not in some vague immortality of the soul but in a resurrection of the body, by which he meant the survival and revival of personality. He did, however, reject the idea of pain and suffering as the will of God for his children. In Jesus he found strength and help to overcome what could not be understood.

He proclaimed the need for the Church to breed liberal evangelicals, though his liberalism (like much else in his life) might seem old-fashioned in its style to those whose Christianity means seeking new things rather than seeing all things made new. It is hard, for example, to imagine him flaunting a word like "myth" in the public's face when explaining the

Incarnation, and then protesting in the name of academic freedom and intellectual refinement that his words didn't mean what the plain people took them to mean. Yet it is equally difficult to align him with some of the strong conservative trends of our time. He was admirably equipped to help the "Bible Christians" who ask what the Bible says but he never separated that from the other part of the same question, which is what does the Bible *mean*. His own answers were related not only to his scholarship but to a liberal Protestant tradition that was stronger in Victorian times than our own.

Perhaps he was a very late Victorian, in the sense that he retained and adapted some of the Victorian virtues to meet the needs of a very different time. Perhaps the fairest description of him is as an old-fashioned and evangelical liberal, in whom evangelical enthusiasm came to terms with critical Biblical scholarship. It may be that in religion as in politics an old-fashioned liberal, confronted with a new radicalism which seems to abandon basic assumptions, may have no choice but to risk appearing conservative. If so, it was in that sense that Barclay was theologically conservative.

Yet to call him old-fashioned in anything risks doing him an injustice. His power of personality knew no barriers of age in its appeal. He was a man for all ages as well as for all currents of mainstream Christianity. While he was still writing I carried out some readership research. What was surprising was not that Barclay was far and away the most popular writer with readers but that his appeal crossed so many barriers.

Barclay was a Scot of Scots and (despite his West Highland parentage) a Clydesider at that. But he appealed not only to his own people in the industrial West of Scotland where his own university looks from its hilltop across what remains of the shipyard cranes. He crossed barriers of cultural difference and theological conservatism to make his mark on people in the Outer Isles, where the innermost thoughts and prayers of religion are still in the Gaelic tongue that his own father had known. He appealed to those people there who might still think that they are not "good enough" to take the bread and wine of the Lord's Table. But he communicated too (as Ronald Falconer brings out well in this book) with rough-hewn and roughly spoken urban Scots with a very different lifestyle.

Far more important, however, his marvellous facility for simple communication on a high level extended and still maintains his direct appeal to every country with a Christian community whose first language or *lingua franca* is English, even England itself. His indirect appeal is likely to become even more extended in translation. He has reached not only major European languages but Japanese. At the time this is written negotiations are far advanced for a Russian version of the *Daily Study Bible.*

In an age when Scotland has often seemed introverted and isolated, or when the national image has been created by the Wembley invaders, he had an eager following for his books in England, the United States, and the Commonwealth. Even his magazine series, some of which eventually became books, built up substantial subscription lists in the English Free Church and Anglican ministries. His books were as likely to be on sale in Wells Cathedral as in a Methodist bookshop.

When he died, one of the most moving tributes to him that I read was in the very specialised magazine, edited by nuns, of the Roman Catholic religious orders in Scotland. One of my own most memorable encounters with him was when I was visiting the College Club in Glasgow University and he called me over to meet Bernard Häring, the great teacher of moral theology and medical ethics at the Lateran university in Rome, although for some reason unpopular at the time with the Scottish Roman Catholic hierarchy. Yet when I was myself at odds with ecumenical fashion and the Kirk's Moderator, having said what most of Scotland thought or was saying in private about the canonisation of the seventeenth-century Jesuit John Ogilvie, and the cancer-curing miracle attributed to his intercession with God, it was Willie Barclay who was ready to be quoted when it counted. Some others preferred to whisper non-attributable concurrence.

He was not a timid man and in important things not a shy one, though he said he often kept silent to avoid a quarrel and he was hurt by bitter or unfair criticism. But he was certainly a modest man, perhaps in some things too modest — a thought which occurred to me after reading Johnston McKay's fascinating contribution to this book. He declined the greatest honour which his own Church could bestow on him, the

Moderatorship for a year of the General Assembly, and he would certainly have deplored many of the praises heaped on him since his death. He had even hoped, vainly as it turned out, to avoid the different kinds of public ceremonial with which Christians and universities mark the passing of their dead.

But as a communicator, he would probably have felt that if there had to be such praises there should be some kind of reasoned argument and step-by-step exposition about them.

What he wrote always had a pattern and a logical sequence. One thought, one assumption, one argument seemed to lead logically to the next. Yet it was possible to identify and isolate the stages in his reasoning, even to disagree with some of them without rejecting his conclusion.

That is why I think it is worth trying to analyse some of the reasons, obvious and not so obvious, distinctive of the man or of the people from whom he came, which helped to make Barclay a great Christian communicator.

II: "The elements were so mixed in him . . ."

How shall we set down the things that made Willie Barclay so uncommon a man and distinguish between the elements that were mixed with such distinction in him?

Many of those who read him today, like those who write about him, retain a sense of his power of personality: his manner, his appearance, his mannerisms, and perhaps most of all that clear and excellently articulated yet rather hoarse and rasping Scottish voice. To the English it probably sounded more appropriate to the football terracing than to an intensely classical education. To the Scots themselves it might have been more readily identifiable with the oratory of a Burns Supper than of a pulpit.

But if Barclay was as good a communicator as he seemed to those of us who came face to face with him, he is likely to go on teaching those who never had a chance to know him. What can we say that will make his teaching more effective?

I believe his success had five elements; his personality, his qualifications, his approach, his techniques, and his demonstration of the power of Christian life and belief. Put together, they made him a great communicator of the greatest of all communications.

I hope something of that personality shines through everything written about him in this book — in some cases by those who knew him long and intimately, in others by those who only met him when his pilgrimage had already taken him to the Delectable Mountains, from whose high point it is possible to "see something like the gate and also some of the glory of the place" at the end of the journey. In one case, quite deliberately, the impression of his personality and power of communication has been sought from an American admirer — also a distinguished academic — who never met him.

Barclay had a natural gift for compelling attention and for carrying conviction. It would have served him well if he had chosen to sell second-hand cars or insurance. Perhaps it is best to let all that is written in this book convey in different ways the intangible as well as the identifiable things that made up that personality. There is, however, one thing that needs to be said. The personality that he expressed in his later communication as professor and public presence had been developed, tested, and matured in the unspectacular private and pulpit communication of the parish ministry. He had learned what passed over people's heads and how they responded.

His experience bore out what another great Scottish university man of his time, the theologian Tom Torrance, has said about the Christian ministry. The most effective preaching is linked to being a diligent pastor. To reach people you have to get to know them. When you really know them you may want to reach them in a different way. And when you have reached them with your preaching the pastoral relationship can be deepened and strengthened.

The years Barclay spent as a parish minister in Renfrew, next door to Glasgow, were not wasted or lost years. They were the years when he developed his gift of communication, starting with Sunday school teachers' material, but they also gave him experience of reaching the people with whom he never lost touch, the silent majority of Christians at the back of the church and on the fringe of the Church.

Until recently, at least, the tradition of Presbyterian Churches in the Scottish tradition was that their scholars moved into the universities from the parish ministry. That was true of Thomas Chalmers and such great Victorians as A. H. Charteris and Robert Rainy and, in our own time, of Tom Torrance. Thanks to modern developments in the universities it is ceasing to be true, and whether that will be good for either the Church or for academic life remains to be seen.

Barclay, in keeping with this tradition, kept up his scholarship. He was a classical and New Testament Greek scholar of distinction and was well established in the life of his university before his name became widely known in the Church and to the much wider public, who knew and loved him during the last twenty-five years of his life. No doubt (as more than one contribution to this book suggests) he then encountered some jealousy from fellow academics, just as he did from some of those still doing his own previous kind of work in the parish ministry.

But in every generation a number of able men and women have these qualifications, often with considerable power of personality and the ability to share their Christian faith as well as their scholarship with their students. Why did Barclay make such a dramatic breakthrough in communicating so much more widely?

Before giving his techniques and approach their due it may be right to recognise that the time was favourable. The postwar years, from 1945 to some time in the early 1960's, showed the Churches to be surprisingly resilient. In all the main West European languages major, and on the whole successful, attempts were made to render the Bible in contemporary speech. Others with special gifts, such as J. B. Phillips and E. V. Rieu (and later C. H. Rieu), made a considerable impact which could in some things be compared with Barclay's. The generation which had fought the war supplied a good flow of recruits for the ministry in all the major Churches and filled the opportunities open to them as laymen. Laywomen began to move out of the tea-tent into a wider field and those Churches which did not ordain women to the ministry (or even at that time the eldership in the Church of Scotland) found themselves under pressure to do so.

There was a massive expansion both in secondary and in university education, with many of those best able to take advantage of the new opportunities coming from social groups where the Churches remained strong and to which they had looked for elders, local preachers, deacons, and Sunday school teachers as well as ministers. Radio had challenged some of the supremacy of the printed word in communication but on the whole it was an ally, not an enemy, both of serious reading and religion, as well as of good music. When Barclay drew an analogy between appreciating Beethoven's Ninth Symphony and discovering the riches of the New Testament he wrote for a generation which had had a good deal of its musical and general education from BBC radio broadcasting.

Only in one respect was the timing of events against him. Although there is a working translation of the New Testament interspersed in the *Daily Study Bible* his definitive new translation did not appear until 1968–69. By then the *New English Bible*'s New Testament had been available for seven years (and had sold four million copies in its first year alone). The main impact of Phillips and of E. V. and C. H. Rieu was even earlier. In the years immediately before Barclay's translation appeared there had also been the very well received Roman Catholic Jerusalem Bible, found on many Protestant shelves, and the New Testament *Today's English Version* — or *Good News for Modern Man*.

It is not entirely facetious to suggest that by then modern man, even if eager to read the Bible, did not regard a new translation as quite such good news as it had been even a few years earlier. F. F. Bruce in his *History of the Bible in English* (Lutterworth Press, 1979 edition) recognises Barclay as a "prince of communicators" and claims that he "never exercised his gift to better purpose". Others might think that Barclay was so much the scholar here that at times he sacrificed his own powers of English style, which were considerable, though he powerfully revived, for example, a fine old English word that has perhaps retained more force in its Scottish usage: In the *New English Bible* Peter is "hurt" when Jesus, after the Galilee fish-breakfast this side of the Resurrection, asked him for the third time about his love. In the Authorised Version he is grieved. Barclay has: "Peter was vexed that Jesus said to him a third time 'Do you love me'," using the colloquial Scots idiom and keeping the strength of the A.V. style.

I doubt if the translation has had the use and recognition that it merited. Perhaps the reason is a feeling that a committee job is somehow holier than a personal one, but probably it has been mainly the matter of timing.

But for about fifteen or twenty years before Barclay's definitive translation appeared he had been a major Christian communicator. His first success was with what might be called the upper end of his own home market, plain but thinking (and reading) men and women — many of them local congregational leaders, Sunday school and Bible class leaders, and Boys' Brigade officers. The majority of them, to begin with at least, were probably people of his own background and style, strongly attached to the Church and highly literate, though sometimes in skilled manual rather than professional work. His years as a parish minister, however, dealing pastorally with people who were very passive listeners to sermons or who rarely came to church, even people who came to church only for weddings and funerals, gave him an understanding of the other end of the home market. This also opened the way for him eventually to use television to reach many people who read few books on anything and none on religion. While he was extending his influence outside Scotland among the local leaders of the Church he was extending his influence within Scotland to people who remained on its fringe.

His success on radio was steady, sure and predictable. What was quite unpredictable, and possible only because of the help and insight of exceptional professional broadcasters, especially Ronald Falconer, was that success on TV. For once the broadcasters saw that the truest professionalism was not to impose their own techniques or some BBC notion of what a TV personality ought to look like and sound like. His role as broadcaster, however, deserves special analysis. (See Chapter 8.) What needs to be said at this stage is that a large part of his success in broadcasting grew from the same root as much of his success as a popular writer on a high level. He had a gift which was not just for a lucid approach which always sounded logical, and usually was. He also knew how to teach without talking down to his pupils.

After I had written that last paragraph I discovered that he himself had once summed up his advice to aspiring broadcasters as "never under-rate your audience". His technique, which involved the efficient preparation made possible by a remarkable range of reading and power of memory, seems to me to have been unconsciously based on applying that principle to every audience, in his private conversation, and his writing and teaching.

He also recognised, in a way that many younger Christian preachers and communicators have failed to do, that the minister of word and sacrament today often has many people in his congregation whose general education matches or even surpasses his own and that the general level of education and public awareness in the community means that people have lost much of the old interest in what a preacher thinks about economics, politics, or science. Just at the time when many other clergymen were eager to pronounce on politics and economics, Barclay's recognition of this challenge to some kinds of pulpit authority helped shape his own approach to preaching and teaching. But it fitted in well with an older Scottish tradition, perhaps most marked in the United Free Church before its reunion with the other half of Scottish Presbyterianism, though its ancestry can be traced back to the emphasis given to the Scottish Reformation by John Knox and Andrew Melville. Those old divisions in Presbyterianism scarcely matter today (except among the "Wee Free" remnant who were torn between grudging admiration of Barclay's power as a Bible communicator and abhorrence of his liberalism). But when I and others, not knowing which branch of Presbyterianism Willie Barclay had come from, had to guess before checking up on it, we were able to guess correctly.

In education this Scottish tradition, so closely linked with what might be called the selective democracy of the Reformed Church, has been called that of the "democratic intellect". Willie Barclay's approach to Christian communication was that of the democratic intellect in action.

It might be summed up like this. There is a natural equality, or an equality before God, between professor and students or between minister and people. All Christians are equal in God's love though some know a lot more than others about New Testament Greek, Roman labour relations, civic life in Tarsus, or the going rate for selling sparrows. And some grow faster and further in grace than others.

What is vital, and implicit in Barclay's approach, is the assumption that when academic knowledge has been shared among the people (much as loaves and fishes were in another place) conclusions about the rule of faith and life ultimately depend on a personal relationship with God through Christ and on the informed right of private judgment of the house-wife, the bank clerk, the electrician, and the shipyard worker as well as the professor. There is a significant passage in one of Barclay's books about how utterly baffled an elder, who was a foreman patternmaker, found himself — a cultured as well as an intelligent and skilled man — when taken to join a dis-cussion group of young theologians. It opened up the gap between the professional theologian and the intelligent, thoughtful, articulate layman.

Having probably encountered some of the same young theologians grown a little older, I feel for that pattern-maker — the more so because my father was a patternmaker on Clydeside too. Barclay knew from instinct, experience, and living faith what it took me a long time to learn after exposure to university life and acquiring fluency in a different kind of academic pidgin-language from that of the theologians: that there is a narrow way that avoids either talking down to people or over their heads.

Despite this ability to touch a deep and vital chord in Scottish life and history, however, Barclay was probably a better Christian and a better Protestant (despite that belief in universal salvation that for me raises awkward problems about a Purgatory arranged by God rather than policed by priests) than he was a Presbyterian in the purely literal sense. He was no great attender at the courts of the Church, especially Presbytery. And as Glasgow had some rule about having to attend the Presbytery in order to be sent from it to the General Assembly he was not present as a member in the greatest gathering of the Scottish Kirk for more than twenty years, though he came to receive its heartfelt thanks when he retired from his Chair. He never gave the impression that something should be accepted as true because an ancient council or modern committee said so, and the idea of infallibility of Presbyteries and General Assemblies — happily and explicitly rejected in the classic Presbyterian Westminster Confession — would have appealed no more to him than the infallibility of Italian bishops, or even Polish bishops in translation.

Too much, indeed, should not be made of his special rapport with his own Scots people. Perhaps it was just that he had the rapport with people and was a fairly stay-at-home Scot. Any possibility that he might have changed these stay-at-home ways late in life was ruled out by his health in latter years. I once tried to tempt him with what I hoped might be the serialised great religious best-seller of the century: "Barclay in the Holy Land". He would have licked H. V. Morton and Malcolm Muggeridge to a frazzle, but I discovered it was not temptation. He was kind and polite in turning it down, but not at all attracted.

But while he generally stayed at home, his power of words, explanation, and conviction made him a great communicator across the world. He reached the Americans, for example, without going to them. They came to him, though he went as far as St Andrews for their summer school and they got some golf into the bargain. Even allowing for the American weakness for things Scottish — I can think of at least two leading Scottish churchmen, for example, who seem to make a greater impact today in the United States than they do at home in the Kirk — this was a remarkable achievement for a man with no passion for dollar fees and no inclination to go on lecture circuits. But he had the same impact in English-speaking countries elsewhere, including Third World countries; and as Ronald Falconer shows later in this book, even his late success on television extended to the Antipodes. There is a very particular example, also in this book, of what that success could mean in changing the life of a man in a Government position on the other side of the world — and that, so it may seem to believers, may be more than coincidence.

What was the technique that served him so well, and let him

serve others? It depended on that vast reference library and filing cabinet of his learning and reading. Quite unself-consciously on a typical page he would enlist arguments and analogies not only from the Old and New Testaments but from Shakespeare on Falstaff's death, Brecht in *Mother Courage*, Seneca, and Clarence Day in *Life with Father*. It was enlivened by his wit, gentle and rich in kindness, and his never-failing flow of apt allusions and analogy. It was a part of his person-ality — as when he capped John's revelation of Heaven as having no more sea with one of his own (and was it not in a way inspired too?) when he said that for breathless people like him it would have no more stairs. Yet some of what he set down as self-analysis — such as his conviction that if you got the first sentence right everything else flowed from it — might frus-trate anyone who tried to imitate him.

I am inclined to think that he was able to develop this technique because early in his life he had got his relationship with his readers and audiences right — though I wish he had written more about what it was like in the 1930's to come back from Marburg to Renfrew. I am also inclined to think that like many of us he unconsciously modelled himself on teachers and professors he admired, and that he enjoyed a great age of Scottish high school teaching and a golden age of professorial lecturing at Glasgow University. I remember the insight that I had into a golden age of British politics when, after hearing Churchill in his Indian summer, I was able to meet Lady Violet Bonham-Carter and hear her lecture. It suddenly dawned on me: perhaps in Asquith's day they were all eloquent like that! Perhaps to some extent in Willie Barclay we encountered the golden sunset of a golden age, a tradition of lecturing, one that among other things mastered the art of including quotation without destroying the character and flow of the lecturer's own style and message.

Some purists might say Barclay quoted too much. But surely no-one quoted so well. It would be wrong to say he didn't quote for effect, but he certainly didn't use that astonishing catholicity of knowledge to show off. Indeed he did happily display tastes like J. M. Barrie which trendier academics might share but would discreetly conceal. The effect he cared about was on the reader and listener — the effect he wanted was not to impress but to help.

This expertise and personality, however, do not tell the whole story. Perhaps in industrial Saxony or in the Donbas coalfield there is someone, rooted in the region, who has exceptional gifts of lucidity and clarity in making Marx comprehensible and Lenin attractive to those who have been conditioned to believe in them. Given the tedium of Marx and the character of Lenin, such ideological professors may need even more technical skill and special aptitude than Barclay if they can communicate as effectively wherever German or Russian are languages of explanation and exhortation.

Barclay was a great communicator, but only because he believed in his communication. He spoke not just with his lips — or from his throat — but with his heart. And he never spoke more convincingly of the unique power and nature of Jesus Christ than on occasions when some fundamentalists thought he was rejecting their idea of "Bible Christianity". For all his scholarship, talent and wisdom, his communication had the extra dimension that Christians believe comes from God through Jesus Christ, not only the way and the life but God's truth.

Perhaps he was no theologian, or so I am told. He said so himself, and his judgment is supported by those who agree with him and each other on very little else. Some of those who usually agreed with him and always loved him agreed on that point too. One of them, now sharing the same reception for the saints, warned me against ever giving him a platform for his views on the Old Testament and insisted: "Don't on any account let him give you a series on the Atonement."

He had enemies as well as critics and he aroused jealousies. Since more than one contributor to this book mentions the academic jealousies it is right to testify that there were ordinary hard-working parish ministers who envied his success too and couldn't see that he had anything that they hadn't — except such a vast congregation. I have sniffed these sour grapes from both liberal and conservative wings of the Church, sometimes flavoured with academic comments about being "thirty-five years out of date in his scholarship". At its most rational, such criticism claimed that Barclay as a communicator avoided some of the more difficult problems of

New Testament scholarship and ignored difficulties that could spoil many a simple Christian's understanding of John's Gospel or some of the Epistles.

The weight of such criticism depends, perhaps, on whether one thinks that thirty-five years' accumulation of scholarship makes a great difference to the plain man and woman's understanding of the Christian Gospel.

As the contemporary Scots Christian poet George Bruce wrote recently of the "stylometry" which sets computers to work on the Epistles (as well as Shakespeare's plays) it may not matter very much whether the signature appended to a letter was that of Paul when (as in the great hymn of love in Corinthians) "the most evident hand is that of Jesus Christ".

All that Barclay wrote on the New Testament sought to make evident the hand of Jesus Christ, and reflected the way that He was Barclay's own guide. And no problem which remains about the way the New Testament message was set down surely matches the problem of mind and heart which has been overcome to find — as the hymn says, "a thing most wonderful, *almost* too wonderful to be" — when Jesus Christ is accepted as the saving way to see God, and find forgiveness.

That is what I believe Barclay communicated. More than anyone in his time I believe that he showed the depths of experience and teaching, as well as of love, which are found in the four brief Gospels and the handful of books and letters which accompany them in the New Testament. For the God he saw in Jesus Christ is not a metaphor associated with a myth, but the personal, provident, creating and loving God of Scripture and Christian experience, the Father seen through the Son. And if Barclay had problems with the Third Person of the Trinity, and found it hard to distinguish between Risen Christ and Holy Spirit, he probably shared them with a great company of the believing Christians of every century.

Communication is a part of the Communion of the saints, or at least has a vital part in creating the community which is a foretaste of it. Those who give their testimony in this book to Barclay's skills, talents, personality, and faith (with some weaknesses, limitations, and blind spots) show how Christian communication is linked to Christian community.

As I read back over what I have written to introduce their

very different contributions, and think about what they have written, I wonder if we have made Barclay seem a saint.

Of course he was not what the world considers a saint. Saints, being ascetics if not always teetotallers, surely never even sniff whisky. They do not talk about enjoying life. Saints, haloed and constrained, laugh less than Willie Barclay and speak with less bite and more caution. At least some traditional saints of Latin and Greek Christendom do: I am not so sure about Columba.

But in one sense I hope I have made him seem a saint, not specially a saintly person but one who belonged on earth to the community of Christ in a way which promised well for heaven.

The old Presbyterian catechism lists the enjoyment of the communion of saints as one of the special privileges of the visible Church. Willie Barclay's style and mood did not always fit in well with that stern catechism or the Westminster Confession on which it is based. But the Confession speaks of saints — that is, those united to Christ — being also united to one another in love and having "communion in each other's gifts and graces".

It is a happy and blessed as well as a noble phrase.

Many of us in one way or another had communion in Barclay's special gifts and graces. Through them we enjoyed a warmer community. Millions of people were helped through the power of communication which he used in the interest of Christian communion. This book may show not only that many people remain grateful but that many more people can still be helped.

3 – Barclay's message, in his own words . . . On Mark, Bible-reading, Romans and Gambling

In the chapters which follow, the editor's interpolations and notes are in italics. Everything else is by the contributors whose names appear at the head of the chapters.

But there seemed something missing even when these moving, fascinating, analytical, and often very personal testimonies or arguments which follow had been set out in order: something else that needed to be fitted in.

For those who knew Barclay, even by reputation or through his books, there is no problem. But someone somewhere is going to be moved by chance, or by God's guidance, to browse through the book. There is a danger that it is going to sound like having to listen to the speeches at someone else's club dinner or school reunion. "This Barclay", the response may be, "seems to have been quite a guy" — or even, where the browser's idiom is different, "a pretty interesting chap really. But what did this wonderful gift for communication really amount to; what did it sound like?"

What needed to be fitted in was a taste of Barclay himself, not purple passages but the kind of communication character-istic of him. I have therefore chosen a piece which is of historical and biographical importance, two pieces from Barclay's late prime, and one from the last magazine series he wrote, not about the New Testament but about Christian ethics. They show the consistency as well as the clarity of the style. Those who read them will learn something about Barclay from his style and approach. Perhaps they will also learn something about the things that he cared for and lived to communicate.

I: How to begin the Bible

The first Barclay piece was written while he was only in his second year as a lecturer at Glasgow University but it reflects his long experience in communicating the Gospel as a parish minister, for Sunday schools, and with the Boys' Brigade. It appeared in the Church of Scotland's magazine Life and Work *in January 1948 as the start of a series by Barclay — identified only as "W. Barclay" — called "Beginning again". It was meant by the then editor Jack Stevenson (one of those who early recognised Barclay's great talents) as a page for those who wished to find their way into Bible-reading and to relate it to their lives. It asked them to start with Mark's Gospel.*

Read Chapter 1 in sections and as a whole this month *wrote Barclay, adding a note about a question-asking technique at the end of the piece which was to become characteristic of him.* Try to answer the questions honestly.

Note how the very first verse of the Gospel is a declaration of Mark's faith — the Gospel of Jesus Christ, *the Son of God*. It is sometimes demanded that we should give a detached unprejudiced account of the life of Jesus; but it has been said that a biographer can only produce a notable biography if he either loves or hates his subject. Mark was not ashamed to show at the outset that he was "prejudiced" in favour of Jesus. Are we too much concerned in religion to keep all the arguments in balance, and too much ashamed of our convictions, when we are not ashamed of strong convictions elsewhere — e.g., in politics? Do we who are Christians sometimes *argue* too much and *witness* too little?

Verses 2–9 indicate to us that God had been steadily throughout the ages preparing the world to receive Jesus Christ. As God leads and guides men into truth, He gives them just as much as they can at any one stage understand and is always preparing them for another stage. *Are there any signs of this happening in our own lives just now*? What seems to be the next thing God is trying to teach us? What does it mean to take upon ourselves full allegiance to Jesus Christ? Are we helping to prepare others to take that step?

Verses 14 and 15 tell us the message with which Jesus came to men. Jesus came to preach the good news of *the Kingdom*. What is the Kingdom of God? In His prayer Jesus taught us to pray: "Thy Kingdom come; Thy will be done in earth as it is in heaven." The second phrase explains the first. The Kingdom is a society in which both for the individual and for the society as a whole the will of God is the only law. Do we talk too much of *political* necessities and *economic* necessities and *social* necessities and too little of the *divine* necessities which should be our real law? What differences might it make in our country if we were concerned first about what *God* thinks necessary? And in our own lives — what, in His view, is most urgently necessary?

In this chapter, right at the beginning of His ministry, Jesus is shown engaged in two great activities: (1) He is engaged in a *teaching activity*. Verse 21 tells that He went into the synagogue *and taught*. Verses 38 and 39 show Him setting out on a tour of the synagogues to preach and teach, and declaring that that was the very object of His coming. He came to tell men the truth about God and about themselves. *Are we putting ourselves in the position to be taught what He has to tell us*? If His teaching work is to go on He needs voices to speak for Him. Are you doing your part within the Church, for example in the Sunday School, to help Christ in this task? Is the Church as a whole accepting its task of *teaching*, not only its members but the whole world, the Christian truth? (2) He is engaged in a *healing activity*. Verses 23–26, 30–34, 40–42 show Jesus engaged in healing. Clearly Jesus is showing that the Kingdom of God not only involves that men's *minds* should be instructed but that their *bodies* should be healthy and strong. The work that goes on in the hospital ward or the doctor's surgery is a sacred work. Isn't that a challenge to our usual way of dividing life into compartments? What does that say to us, to the Church, to the State? Should there be a closer alliance between the Church and the work of healing? Does the Church face as it should the social task which it must face if it is to assist in bringing in the Kingdom?

This chapter shows Jesus from the very beginning of His ministry strengthening Himself from two sources of power: (1)

Verse 10 tells of "the Spirit" descending upon Him. Read through the book of Acts and note how every great decision was taken in the guidance of the Spirit. The Spirit cannot be *won*; it must be *asked for and received*. Is there enough asking and waiting upon God in our lives? (2) Verse 35 shows us Jesus at prayer. Do we really believe that "more things are wrought by prayer than this world dreams of"? At the back of our feverish activity is there this central determination to keep in living touch with God for guidance and correction?

Read this chapter again. Think now what "The Kingdom of God" means, and what is the method of its coming.

II How to see the shining light

More than twenty years later Barclay had a world reputation as a Christian writer, especially in helping people to get the most from their reading of the New Testament. This general introduction to one of his series on the New Testament — "The Men, the Meaning, the Message of the Books" — first appeared in 1971 in Life and Work.

It contains some characteristics of Barclay's style — for example in the way that every word tells in the analogy with listening to Beethoven's Ninth Symphony and in the quite unselfconscious demonstration of Barclay's remarkable memory and range of reading.

Then as an example of the approach to the New Testament which Barclay outlined there follows his handling, a few months later, of "Paul's greatest letter", the Epistle to the Romans.

In his book *How to read the Bible* F. C. Grant tells of an experience which happened to a friend of his. His friend had been giving an address to a group of people on how to read the Bible. No sooner had he finished than a young woman rose and said "You don't need someone to tell you how to read the

Bible. Open it anywhere, read three verses, make your mind a blank, and the Holy Spirit will do the rest!"

For a point of view like that there is no such thing as Bible *study*.

Benjamin E. Mays, the great negro educator, in his book *Born to Rebel,* tells how in his young days among many of the negroes there was an actual prejudice against education. He himself in the end had to defy his own father to get his education. The attitude was that "God *called* men to preach, and when he called them, he would tell them what to say!" Education, study, were superfluous.

No-one is going to deny that the simplest and the most unlettered person, with no aids to study at all, can find the word of God in the Bible, and can discover there strength for life, comfort for sorrow, and guidance for action. But it is also true that the more we bring to the Bible, the more we will get from the Bible.

There is more than one level at which we may listen to anything. Take the case of music. We may listen to a great symphony simply as a marvellous river of sound. That is the simplest way of listening. We may study the programme notes, and we may see the structure of the music. We may see how the themes enter and are developed and interwoven by the composer. That brings something more to the study of the music. We may, before we listen, find out something about the life and experience of the composer, so that we know something of the situation out of which the music was born. That clearly will make the music more meaningful yet.

Take the case of Beethoven's Ninth Symphony. We may listen to it, knowing no more than that this is sound and melody which thrills the ear and speaks to the heart. We may study the programme notes, and we can hear the pattern of the music developing, as we listen for the entry of each instrument and the development of each theme. Before we come to the performance, we can learn something of the life of Beethoven, and we can become aware that it was out of the prison of total deafness that Beethoven wrote that symphony, and that he never heard it except in his mind. To know *that* will make listening to that symphony one of the most moving experiences that music can bring.

The Bible is like this. Of course, the simplest person can open it and read it. But the more we know about the Bible, the more thrilling and fascinating this book becomes. Kipling in one of his poems writes:

> I keep six honest serving-men
> (They taught me all I knew);
> Their names are What and Why and When
> And How and Where and Who.

In the opening lines of his *Introduction to First Peter*, F. J. A. Hort writes: "To understand a book rightly, we want to know who wrote it, for what readers it was written, for what purposes, and under what circumstances." In other words, we need to call in Kipling's six honest serving-men when we want really and fully to study any book, and to study the Bible. Let us look at some of the questions, even if in our space we cannot look at them all. It matters very much *who* says a thing.

I remember once being at a concert at which a baritone came on and sang Henley's *Invictus*.

> Out of the night which covers me,
> Black as the pit from pole to pole,
> I thank whatever gods there be
> For my unconquerable soul.

As the man turned to leave the platform after singing, I suddenly saw what I had not noticed when he came on. *He was blind*. It makes a difference when a blind man can sing that.

We read in Romans (8:28): "We know that in everything God works for good". This would not be a very impressive saying from one on whom the cold wind had never been allowed to blow. But the man who said it was the man who had, not the thorn, but the stake (*skolops*) turning and twisting in his flesh and making life an agony (2 Corinthians 12:7). When a man can never be free of pain, and yet affirm that in his experience God does all things well — this means something. It matters very much *when* a thing is said.

It was "in the year that King Uzziah died" that Isaiah had his vision — and that was a year of tragedy (Isaiah 6:1). Uzziah or Azariah had been one of the great and good kings. But in one reckless moment he had insisted on himself burning incense in the temple, and then and there he had become a leper. That was the year in which the splendour of the king had finished up in a lazar house (2 Kings 15:1–5; 2 Chronicles 26:16–21). As George Adam Smith puts it: "The king sank into a leper's grave, but before Isaiah's vision the divine majesty arose in all its loftiness." To have the vision of God in a sunlit time would no doubt be great, but to have vision of God when life is shot through with sheer tragedy is greater yet — and that is what Isaiah had. It matters very much *where* a thing is said.

One of the great things that Paul said is in the letter to the Corinthians: "Neither the immoral, nor adulterers, nor idolaters, nor homosexuals, nor thieves, nor greedy, nor drunkards, nor revilers, nor robbers, will inherit the kingdom of God. *And such were some of you*" (1 Corinthians 6:9, 10). Corinth was the city with the temple of Aphrodite which had a thousand priestesses who were sacred prostitutes, and who came down to the city streets to ply their trade each evening, so that the Greeks had a saying, "It is not everyone who can afford a journey to Corinth." It was commonly said that no Corinthian was ever introduced in a play on the stage other than blind drunk. There was a Greek verb *korinthiazesthai*, which derived from the name Corinth, which means to indulge in drunken revelry. The letter begins with an address to "the church of God which is at Corinth" (1 Corinthians 1:2). The church of God which is at *Corinth* — Bengel's comment is, "a huge and happy paradox". It was not in some respectable part of suburbia that the grace of God operated mightily — it was at *Corinth*.

It can often happen that the simple placing of an incident in its context sheds a new light on it. Take the case of the incident in which James and John, or their mother, seek to gain from Jesus a guarantee of the chief places when he comes into his kingdom. (Matthew 20:20, 21; Mark 10:35–37). This is often quoted as an example of the earthly ambition of the disciples, and of their inability to think except in terms of an earthly kingdom. Maybe it is. But it is something more. It is one of the greatest examples of faith in all the gospel story. Jesus was on his way to Jerusalem; it was clear that there was going to be a head-on clash with the Jewish authorities. He had told them again and again of the cross which loomed ahead; but the James and John who made this request could not think of Jesus in any other terms than in terms of ultimate triumph. This may have been a request of ambition, but it was also the request of men whose faith in Jesus was unshaken, even when the storm clouds were gathering.

No-one is going to deny that anyone can read the Bible. But not only to read it but also to study it will make it shine with a new light. It makes all the difference *who* said a thing; it makes all the difference *when* it was said; it makes all the difference *where* it was said.

For some time to come we will be, I hope, studying the New Testament together. The method which I propose to use is this. I think that it is possible to find in each book of the New Testament one basic, dominant idea. I think that it is possible in each book to find one special thing which that book was written to say. Of course, there is much more than one idea even in the shortest and the simplest books; but at the heart of each book there is one idea which is the moving cause of the whole matter.

III Paul's greatest letter

There will be none to dispute that the Letter to the Romans is Paul's greatest letter. Many great tributes have been paid to it. E. J. Goodspeed called it "awe-inspiring". Luther said of it, "Romans contains in itself the plan of the whole scripture, and is a most complete epitome of the New Testament or Gospel." Melanchthon, Luther's friend, called it "a compendium of Christian doctrine". To understand Romans is to go far towards understanding Paul.

When Paul wrote it, he was poised upon a great decision. One of Paul's dearest schemes was the collection for the church at Jerusalem from the younger churches (2 Corinthians 8 and 9). That collection had been made, and Paul was just about to leave for Jerusalem with it and with the delegates of the churches which had contributed to it (Acts 20:4). But after the collection had been delivered, Paul had a plan. It was his purpose to visit Spain (Romans 15:24–29).

Spain in the far west was a new territory for Paul, and if he was to launch an invasion of Spain for Christ, he needed a base of operations, and the natural basis was Rome. Paul had always been haunted by Rome. When he set out on his last journey to Jerusalem, he says: "After I have been there, I must see Rome also" (Acts 19:21). When the clouds were gathering during the last days in Jerusalem, the Lord stood by him in the night, and said to him: "Take courage, for as you have testified about me at Jerusalem, so you must bear witness also at Rome" (Acts 23:11). Paul was well aware that the journey to Rome was fraught with danger (Romans 15:30–33). In point of fact, it ended in his arrest, and in the imprisonment from which he was never to be set free. He never reached Spain; he never paid that visit to Rome; it was as a prisoner under arrest that some time later he was to reach Rome. But Paul, when he wrote the Letter to the Romans, had never been in Rome. He wanted Rome as a basis for his dreamed-of expedition to Spain. And therefore he wrote to the church at Rome a letter setting out his faith, so that they might see what kind of a man he was, and what kind of a faith he held, and so be ready to help and support him, when he set out for the far west.

In *Romans*, Paul concentrates on two closely related subjects — the relationship of man to God and the relationship of man to man. In the Gentile world the relationship between God and man had broken down. The first chapter of Romans is a terrible indictment of the pagan world with its false wisdom, its idolatry, its homosexuality, and its immorality (Romans 1:18–32).

Nor was the Jewish world any better. The Jews have the law, and the law is holy, just and good, but they have it only to disobey it (Romans 2). All have sinned, and all fall short of the glory of God (Romans 3:23). Sin's grip is on the world. And the trouble is that the law, which was designed to be a defence from sin, can be the very thing that kindles sin.

This is the subject of that piece of tortured biography in

Romans 7. "Apart from the law sin lies dead . . . When the commandment came, sin revived and I died; the very commandment which promised life proved to be death to me" (Romans 7:8–10). "If it had not been for the law, I should not have known sin. I should not have known what it is to covet, if the law had not said 'You shall not covet.'" (Romans 7:7). The trouble is that the law does two things. First, the law defines sin; it lays down what sin is. But second, no sooner is a thing forbidden than it is desired — this is the way of human nature — and, therefore, the law by a tragic paradox begets sin. Turn to the Gentile world, turn to the Jewish world, sin is in control.

But the matter is worse than that. It is in Romans that we meet the doctrine of original sin. Original sin does not mean the tendency to sin; it does not mean an inherited predisposition to sin; it means quite and totally literally that in Adam all sinned — you and I sinned. This is the ancient conception of solidarity. We are individualists; but in the ancient world the individual hardly existed. A man thought of himself, not as an individual, but as a member of a family, a clan, a nation. When Achan sinned, they killed him and his sons and his daughters and his animals and killed them all (Joshua 7). So the doctrine of the original sin holds that because of this solidarity all men literally sinned in Adam.

The basis of the doctrine is in Romans 5:12–14. It can be outlined in a series of steps.

i. The cause of death is sin.
ii. Adam disobeyed a positive command of God, the command not to eat of the forbidden tree.
iii. Therefore Adam died.
iv. Where there is no law to break there can be no sin.
v. Between Adam and Moses the law did not yet exist, because God had not yet given the law.
vi. Although there was no law to break between Adam and Moses men continued to die.
vii. Why? Because all men had literally sinned in Adam, and therefore all had to die.

What is to happen? Man, Jew and Gentile, is helpless. So God in Jesus Christ steps in. If there can be solidarity with Adam, there can be solidarity with Jesus Christ. If man is identified with the sin of Adam, he can be identified with the obedience of Jesus Christ. The terrible process begun in Adam can be reversed in Christ (Romans 5:15–21).

How can this be? By faith. And what is faith? Faith is doing what Abraham did — it is taking God at his word (Romans 4:16–25), accepting God's commands, believing in God's promises, certain that God means, and can do, what he says. And faith is far older than circumcision and the law, for Abraham was right with God before ever he was circumcised and centuries before the law was given to Moses. So God comes to each man, and says in Jesus Christ: "Take me at my word."

What happens when we take God at his word? When that happens we are *justified*. It is clear that Paul is using the word *justify* in a special sense. He talks of God as the one who justifies the ungodly (Romans 4:5). If in modern language I justify myself or someone else, I produce reasons to prove that I or the other person was right to act as I or he did. Now God is not going to produce reasons to prove that the sinner is right to be a sinner. What then does *justify* mean? In Greek the verb to *justify* is *dikaioun*. Greek verbs which end in *-oun* do not mean to make a person something; they mean to treat, reckon or account someone as something. So when it is said that God justifies the sinner it means that *God treats the sinner as if he had been a good man*. It means that though we are hell-deserving sinners God still loves us; it means that not even our sin can separate us from God. It means, in a word, that the relationship between us and God is the relationship between father and son in Jesus' parable of the Prodigal Son.

To be justified by faith is to take God at his word that for the sake of Jesus Christ he will treat me as a beloved son, sinner though I am, if I come to him (Romans 3 and 4). This is what we mean by the *grace* of God. And now there is another problem which Paul deals with in Romans 6. "Are we to continue in sin that grace may abound?" (Romans 6:1). Someone comes to Paul and says: "You say that God's grace is the greatest thing in the world?" "Yes." "You say that God's grace can forgive any sin?" "Yes." Then comes the answer:

"If that is so, let's go on sinning, for the more we sin, the more chances we give this wonderful grace to operate. Sin is a good thing for sin produces grace."

Paul's answer is that to speak like that is to show that we do not know what Christianity is all about. For Paul, baptism was adult baptism and baptism was instructed baptism and baptism was, if possible, baptism by immersion. In baptism (Romans 6:3–11) we, as it were, die with Christ, when we plunge below the water, and rise with him, when we rise from the water; and thus we leave the old life behind, and set out on a life that is new. To put it much more simply, how can we go on sinning, when we look at the cross, and say: "God loved me like that"?

Romans chapters 9 to 11 deals with another of the great problems, the problem of why the Jews rejected the Messiah when he came and the problem of their ultimate fate. In chapter 9 Paul begins with the grim statement that the Jews rejected the Messiah, because God willed it and arranged it so; but that is not the end of the story. For he goes on to show that the plan of God is that in the end the Gentiles should bring in the Jews, and that in the end of the day all would be saved. "God has consigned all men to disobedience that he may have mercy on all" (Romans 11:32). Temporary rejection was designed to end in universal salvation. In chapters 12 to 15 Paul turns to the ethical duty of the Christian, and shows men their duty to each other, their duty to the state, and their duty to the weaker brother. The soaring theology of the first eleven chapters is in Paul's invariable way brought to the service of everyday work and life and living. So in this greatest of letters Paul lays down the way to a right relationship with God and a right relationship with each other.

As he usually did in these teaching series, Barclay ended with "Questions for Discussion". They were:

i. Can a modern man really accept the doctrine of original sin in the form in which Paul presents it? What is the essential truth which that doctrine really stands for?

ii. In Romans 9 Paul uses the analogy of the potter (Romans 9:19–23). He takes it from Jeremiah 18:1–6. Is this really a satisfactory analogy? Can we think of God making and breaking men as a potter makes and breaks the vessels made of clay? Can we believe that God will ever treat men as *things* to be made and broken as he wishes? Does this agree with the idea of God as father?

iii. What do we mean by faith? How much of faith consists in believing that certain things are true (accepting a creed), and how much of faith consists in believing in a person (believing that what Jesus says and claims is true)? How much of faith is encounter with, and committal to, a person?

iv. Read Romans 12, 13, 14, 15 and work out what a Christian's duty is (a) to the community; (b) to the state; (c) to the weaker brother; (d) to the person who holds different opinions from his.

IV A Puritan who enjoyed life

To round off this chapter on Barclay through his own writing I move to a quite different demonstration of his clarity and logical sequence of exposition, flavoured this time with a strong taste of the Protestant ethic — and in particular the ethics (or lack of them) in gambling. It comes in April 1975 from his last major magazine series on "Religion and Life".

It shows the ways in which Barclay could marshal even a few, simple, salient facts and rely on reference books. He was big enough to be able to admit in teaching when he drew on other people's work. He was also a lover of life who enjoyed things that were pure and of good report, but he had a strong streak of Victorian puritanism in him (even quoting the not especially puritanical Disraeli). Perhaps I should add that a later analysis by Barclay of the ethics of journalism had some of the same flavour and a distaste for what the Sun newspaper considers fun. But a journalistic editor must assert some privileges. One is to quote rather selectively Barclay's conviction that newspapers' public services "far exceed" their faults; another is to opt to print the gambling piece.

Gambling is one of the oldest and the most universal of human amusements. Dice have been found dating back to very nearly 2000 B.C. In the fifth century B.C., Isocrates was complaining about the number of young men who spent their time and money in gambling dens. Suetonius tells of Nero playing at dice for bets of four thousand pounds per point. Tacitus tells that among the German tribes there were those with such a passion for gambling that "when all else is lost they stake their personal liberty on the last and final throw, so that the loser faces voluntary slavery".

Gambling had even got its grip on members of the Christian Church, for Tertullian writes in the third century: "If you say that you are Christian, when you are a dice-player, you say you are what you are not, because you are a partner with the world." Gambling is something common to every society and to every generation. Wherein then lies its universal attraction?

1. There is the excitement which gambling lends to life, the thrill of staking everything on the turn of a card, or the fall of the dice; the excitement of waiting for the result of a game or a race on which a bet has been placed. Uncertainty always means excitement, and where the uncertainty is linked to the possibility of profit, the excitement is greatly increased.

2. There is the human desire to get something for nothing, and gambling offers the possibility of large profit for no effort.

3. This is linked with two other things. Gambling offers the possibility of security or of escape.

The working man has always been faced with the living of life in unpleasant surroundings with few of the luxuries and the good things of life; and worse, he has always been subject to the threat of unemployment, during which even the standards which he has succeeded in achieving may be lost. If he could only somehow possess himself of a large sum of money, he could escape from his grim environment; he could get for himself some of the luxuries of life; and above all he could be free from the haunting insecurity which continually threatens him. I personally have no doubt that it was the desire for security and the hope of escape from industrial uncertainty which gave the football pools their attraction in their early days.

4. Closely allied with that, there is the situation in which our present taxation system places us. If a man made £24,000

in any one year by ordinary business methods he would have to pay about £18,000 of it in tax; if he made £100,000, he would have to pay about £86,000 in tax. In other words, we have got into a topsy-turvy system in which gambling presents the only way to real wealth. We live in a system which encourages the gambler and discourages the earner.

5. Allied with the excitement angle of gambling, there is the matter of involvement. The ordinary man will never be wealthy enough to own a racehorse for himself, but, if he has a bet on a horse, there is a sense in which for that race the horse becomes his. The ordinary man will never be good enough to play first league football, but, if he has a bet on a team, he is intimately bound up with the fortunes of that team. His bet, his gamble has involved him personally in the contest. Well, then, what is wrong with all this? First of all, let us glance at the extent of this thing. In 1973 punters laid a record £2,826,675,000 in bets, and the figures for 1974 are likely to break that record and to exceed £3000m. £1000m. was taken in betting shops alone; and the Treasury raked in a sum of £226,134,000 in taxes on betting. On any grounds this is a very considerable element in the national life and economy. Lord Beaconsfield referred to it as "a vast engine of national demoralisation".

Before we begin to criticise gambling, it would be well to have a definition of it. In the *Dictionary of Christian Ethics* (edited by John Macquarrie and published by the S.C.M. Press) E. Rogers begins the article on gambling with the following definition: "Gambling may be defined as the determination of the possession of money or money-values, by the appeal to an artificially created chance, where the gains of the winners are made up at the expense of the losers, and the gain is secured without rendering in service or in value an equivalent of the gain obtained."

In the article on gambling in the Hastings *Encyclopaedia of Religion and Ethics* the following charges are made against gambling.

1. Gambling is unproductive. Money is spent and nothing either in goods or services is produced. Money is therefore wasted because it has produced nothing of use or value. It is laid down that there are three ways only in which money may

properly be obtained. It may be obtained *by gift*, in a situation in which the gift may be the result of admiration or affection, or the result of charity at the sight of need. It may be obtained *by labour*, in a situation in which it is the produce of honest and efficient diligence and toil, and in which it will quite certainly be the product of some useful service to the community. It may be obtained *by exchange*, in a situation in which something of value is given in exchange for the money received, whether in services or in goods. Money gained and lost in gambling fulfils none of these conditions.

2. Gambling is anti-social. Herbert Spencer said that gambling "is a kind of action by which pleasure is obtained at the cost of pain to another. The happiness of the winner implies the misery of the loser." Gambling is therefore "anti-social, egoistic, deteriorative of character, and intrinsically savage".

3. Gambling is a deliberate appeal to the instinctive covetousness which lurks in the heart of every man. It is an invitation to try to get something for nothing, to live in plenty without working for it.

4. Gambling makes chance the dominating factor in life. Life ought to be founded on reason, because man is characteristically a reasonable being, but gambling makes reward depend on chance, and therefore literally makes nonsense of life.

5. Gambling contradicts the whole idea of stewardship. If it is true, as the Christian ethic holds, that we and all men hold all that we have in stewardship from God, then all that we possess must be used as God would use it, for the good of the community, and the gambler certainly does not use his possessions, and he does not help others to use theirs, for the general good of the community. The practice of gambling and the exercise of stewardship cannot go hand in hand.

6. Gambling is addictive. It may begin as a pleasant and occasional thrill; it has a very good chance of finishing as a compulsion. The odds are always against the gambler. He therefore gambles and loses and gambles again to recoup his losses, and he is launched on a slope that will rush him to disaster. Someone who worked in the catering industry told me that the women she employed in the kitchen, the cleaners,

the dishwashers, the waitresses, were unanimous that they would rather that their husbands drank than that they gambled. The man who drank might come home drunk on payday; the man who gambled had a fair chance of coming home penniless, having gambled away his entire wage-packet. Gambling, for those who are characteristically its victims, has a drug-like addictive quality.

It is clear that in the broad issue betting and gambling in the usual senses of the terms are dangerous, and even potentially ruinous, activities. But in discussions about gambling certain special issues often provoke discussion. There is the matter of insurance. Some very scrupulous persons feel that to take out insurance is to gamble. But insurance is a contract entered into after the most careful and scientific calculation of statistical probabilities, which is very different from making something dependent on the fall of the dice or the turn of a card. In insurance I admit that something is statistically likely to happen to me, and I take prudent steps to protect myself and others against the results of it.

There are those who feel that all dealing in stocks and shares is gambling. It may and it may not be. Suppose someone known to me has invented or acquired a process which is likely to meet a public need or demand. Suppose this person has no money of his own wherewith to develop or to market this process and its products. Then suppose that I and others have money which is idle. Because we have confidence in the new process, and in the man who owns it, we provide the money for the process to be used and for its products to be marketed. Then we will expect if the enterprise is successful to reap a reward. This is not a gamble; it is to back one's informed judgment of someone else's enterprise.

There is what is in some ways the most difficult argument of all to meet. What harm is there in a man making a bet of a few pence, the loss of which he can well afford? To this there apply exactly the same principles as apply to any act of gambling. It is an attempt in principle to get something for nothing; for the gambler to win someone will have to lose; because of the addictive quality of gambling the small beginning could be the first step to real addiction.

There was a time when it was common for Church organisations to run raffles, lotteries and the like. In the case of the Church it seems to me not so much wrong as degrading that the Church should have to raise money in such a way, and that the Church has to assume that its members will not give to it unless they have the chance of making something out of the giving. Whatever may be permissible for the world, there are things which it should be beneath the spirit of the Church to touch.

There followed, as with a Barclay Bible series, questions to get discussion under way:

1. Do you agree that the Church and its organisations should have nothing to do with fund-raising by raffles and lotteries and the like?
2. What ought to be the attitude of the Christian to things like the office sweepstake? Is it worthwhile to take a stand or is it quite permissible to conform?
3. What ought to be the Church member's attitude to football pools? Suppose someone won a considerable sum on the pools and then offered the Church a large donation, should that donation be accepted?

But perhaps it would be unfair and unrepresentative to end a chapter in which Barclay speaks through his own words, with an ethical dilemma about football pools. I end instead with an epigrammatic thought, perhaps all that ever took shape of what was probably one of the last major pieces he undertook to write; he wrote in December 1977, promising delivery in February, and with Barclay his agreed deadline was his bond, unless he was struck down by illness. In fact he was struck down by death; and knowing his ways of working with a marvellously efficient stewardship of time I don't expect he ever started it.

Suspecting that he wouldn't feel up to another long series of articles I asked him if he would like to write about the doctrine of the Incarnation, which had run into the controversy provoked by a group of theologians committed to the notion of "myth". To my delight he wanted to tackle the Incarnation and replied: (I keep his use of capital and lower case letters, assuming it was deliberate.)

I would very much like to write the article on the Incarnation because it seems to me the incarnation was meant to make Christianity intelligible and in many cases has gone to make it unintelligible.

Since he was not spared to enlarge the epigrammatic sentence, loyalty to his memory suggests a quotation from what he wrote about Matthew's story of how Mary found herself with child, through the action of the Holy Spirit.

The essence of Matthew's story is that in the birth of Jesus the Spirit of God was operative as never before in the world — *that spirit which he called God's agent in the creation of the world.* It is the Spirit who alone can re-create the human soul when it has lost the life it ought to have. Jesus enables us to see what God is and what man ought to be; Jesus opens the eyes of our minds so that we can see the truth of God for us; Jesus is the creating power amongst men; Jesus is the re-creating power which can release the souls of men from the death of sin.

4 – Barclay's humanity and humility
by James Martin

James Martin is minister of High Cartyne Parish Church in the East End of Glasgow, a few yards off the main road to Edinburgh in an old-established and houseproud council estate. He worked closely with his friend William Barclay in revising and editing the new edition of the Daily Study Bible. *Like Barclay he is a Motherwell man, also going through Dalziel High School and Glasgow University. He has written books on the Resurrection, the problem of suffering, and the Holy Land.*

Like Barclay, he has maintained his support for the Motherwell football team despite his move towards Glasgow's rival temples of football devotion.

When William Barclay died it was a great blow and a deep sorrow to multitudes of people the world over. For one who had been a close personal friend for many years it was a severe loss and I feel the pain still.

William Barclay was one of the great Christians of our time; and when I say "great" I mean just that. Most of us are guilty at times of using words lightly or even carelessly, without taking time to consider whether we really want to say in that specific context what they properly mean. When I apply the adjective "great" to William Barclay, I choose it deliberately.

He was a *great* man and his greatness was displayed in many ways.

It is indicated for one thing by the millions who have had reason to give thanks for what he uncovered for them of the riches of the New Testament and its Gospel. Here, too, I use my word advisedly. I do mean "millions", just as I mean great.

Barclay's *Daily Study Bible* series has itself sold over seven million copies in the English language alone.

William Barclay was a communicator of supreme quality, particularly to the so-called man in the street. I for one believe that no-one in this century has done more to communicate and commend the Gospel of Jesus Christ than he. This was mainly because of his unique ability to make the Bible books easily understandable and extremely interesting to masses of ordinary people. This remarkable gift of his was equally evident both in his speaking and in this writing.

I would like, therefore, to say something about Barclay the communicator; first of all the communicator by means of the written word and then the communicator by means of the spoken word.

I Barclay the Writer

What a mighty work he did with his pen! And what a mighty influence his printed words still exert for Christ and his kingdom!

William Barclay never could himself tell you exactly how many books of his had been published. It was, however somewhere in the region of seventy. In his prime — and his writing prime extended until the last year or two of his life — his output was prodigious. Once, when someone commented on his unexpected absence from the Students' Common Room during the forty-five minutes mid-morning break between lectures, a fellow professor remarked, "He's probably just used the time to write another book."

He wrote at great speed for he made sure it was all in his head and in his heart before he commenced. What is more, he rarely took time to revise what he had written and he never took time to polish it up. I well remember calling upon him one day, in the earlier years of our friendship, in his room at the University. He was tapping away at his typewriter, "Just give me a moment," he said, "till I finish this article. It has to go off today."

He wrote rapidly for a few minutes more, then he extracted the paper from the machine, folded it, placed it in the already addressed envelope beside him, sealed the envelope and turned to speak to me. "Aren't you going to read it over?" I asked in some horror. "Don't let my being here keep you from doing so." "Oh," he said, "It has nothing to do with your being here. I never spend time reading a thing over once I have written it."

This method of his had definite drawbacks, as I found out only too well when I accepted the task of revising for its new edition the seventeen volumes of his *Daily Study Bible* series. I had to put right a whole crop of little grammatical loosenesses and other infelicities. But I have no doubt that this was the correct method for him. He was so anxious to get on with his task of communicating the Good News in print that he simply was not prepared to have precious time taken up with what seemed to him a comparatively unimportant process of embellishment.

Had he done the polishing of his work that most writers consider essential, the world might well have been several Barclay books the poorer and what a loss that would have been.

He was passionately concerned in his writings to make the New Testament message clear and persuasive and this he did in a quite marvellous way. Many thousands owe much to this gift of William Barclay's and his dedicated use of it.

I remember, for instance, a certain young woman, just newly become a communicant member of my congregation, who was admitted to hospital for a lengthy stay. On one of my visits to her I gave her a copy of Barclay's *Daily Study Bible* commentary on the Gospel of St. Matthew. On my next visit Nora greeted me with a radiant face and simply could not thank me enough for my gift.

"Mr Martin," she said, "ever since I took my church membership vows, I have read a portion of St. Matthew's Gospel every day, but it is only since you gave me that book of William Barclay's that I have come to understand it properly, and it has made a wonderful difference to me."

A friend of mine who had emigrated to the United States told me this on a visit back to Britain. "We have a good-going Bible Study in our Presbyterian Church over in the States and we use the Barclay commentaries very often as our basis of study. One of the keenest members of the group is a Roman Catholic lady who came along one night and asked if she could join us. The reason was that she had heard we used the Barclay books and, as she put it, she owed her very Christian faith to reading one of them."

Many people personally known to me have found much help and much blessing through making regular use of Barclay's *Daily Study Bible* commentaries. And it is a well-known fact that many ministers in Scotland — elsewhere too, perhaps — make lavish use of Barclay's writings in the preparation of their sermons. I recall Willie on a radio programme having the question put to him: "Do you object to ministers making use of material from your books for their sermons?" "Of course not," he replied. "That was one of the reasons I wrote them."

William Barclay was criticised in some quarters — and sometimes severely — for being "a populariser of the New Testament". The label was attached to him in scorn but it is really a badge of honour, for he was instrumental in making the New Testament real and relevant, frequently fascinating, too, to a multitude of men and women all over the world. It was said of Jesus that the common people heard him gladly. They could grasp easily what he was talking about and at the same time they recognised that what he had to say was of immense importance. I do not think I am being at all irreverent when I say that William Barclay considered that the highest accolade his books ever received was that millions of people read them gladly.

Many a time I have heard him assert that he was no original thinker and that he regarded himself as a kind of "theological middle-man". His gift, as he himself saw it, was not to initiate new thought but to distil the findings and the thoughts of others into a plain language that plain men and women could readily understand.

William Barclay's gift for this kind of distillation and transmission was not only remarkable; it was, I believe, unique and he employed it diligently and energetically in the cause of his Master, particularly in the exposition of the New Testament. Many thousands of men and women alive today are grateful to him for the help his writings have given them; and a considerable number owe their very souls to reading something of what he wrote.

II Barclay the Preacher and Teacher

William Barclay's unique ability to communicate in a lucid and intelligible fashion that was able at the same time to be always interesting and frequently gripping was evidenced, too, in all his public speaking, whether from the pulpit or from the platform, whether in seminar or in discussion group, whether on radio or on television.

He spoke as he wrote. Rather, it would be more accurate to say, he wrote as he spoke. Anyone who heard him speak in public never had the slightest difficulty thereafter in hearing in his mind William Barclay speak to him the words of any of his books he might be reading.

Pulpit. He was an extremely popular and very effective preacher, even though in latter years he professed not to care much for donning the mantle of preacher. He found it now, he said, much too demanding and much too exhausting; he was one who took his preaching so seriously that it was always an occasion of great cost to himself.

He was not a preacher in the romantic mould. Not for him the once traditional and much vaunted style of Scottish pulpit oratory with its purple passages and frequent dramatic climaxes. Moreover he had a rasping kind of voice once described to me as sounding like "two bricks being rubbed together". Nevertheless, he was, in my judgment, a prince of preachers because he achieved superbly what is surely the chief end of preaching, namely, that it should have an important message to proclaim and that it should communicate that message clearly and convincingly. I frequently had the privilege of seeing and hearing William Barclay at work in the pulpit; he was masterly in the way he could arrest and hold his hearers and convey his message to them in vividly persuasive terms.

He consistently deprecated his stature as a preacher. Time after time I have heard him protest that preaching was not his forte. The fact was, however, that, although he may well have felt less comfortable in the pulpit than on the platform — in later years at least — he was always an excellent preacher in every valid sense of the term.

Platform. On the platform William Barclay was supreme. Here, too, he had a never-failing knack of taking his audience into total captivity right at the outset and keeping them in willing and glad bondage to the end. His style was a racy and conversational one. He spoke rapidly and it was not always easy to keep pace with him. But he always spoke in language that anyone and everyone in the audience could understand. Through it all glowed the warmth of his humanity and of his Christian compassion. He was deeply interested in people; he liked them and was deeply concerned about them. The consequence was that he was able to project himself into their situation and so speak often directly to their needs.

One result of this was his brilliance in the question and answer period that was the appendix to many of his platform appearances. I have never known anyone who matched his faculty for understanding questions from the body of the hall. Times without number he got to the heart of such a question better than the questioner himself understood it. Without fail he would put his finger on what the man was really after and invariably was able to give a lucid and relevant reply.

One of the reasons for the Barclay command in the pulpit, on the platform and in discussion was his practice of meticulous preparation. His style was deceptively relaxed, even casual, but in fact he never stood up to give any sort of address anywhere without having prepared thoroughly. No matter the occasion, whether it was a service in some large church packed to the rafters or a tiny meeting in a small back hall, William Barclay always did his homework assiduously. He came to every occasion knowing exactly what he was going to say and exactly how he was going to say it. In addition, he had steeped himself in his subject so thoroughly that whatever questions might be asked and whatever corner of the field might fall to be explored, he was in absolute command.

III Barclay the Broadcaster

Every one of the qualities I have mentioned had a contribution to make to the enormous success William Barclay achieved as a religious broadcaster first on radio and then on television. There were, of course, other factors adding something to that success which emerged only in the heat of the battle.

He brought to his broadcasting the same thoroughness of preparation which characterised all his public speaking. He never would allow himself to go on the air without being completely ready. This was part of the secret of the colossal impact he made.

It was, however, only part of the secret; there were other factors, too. First, and perhaps foremost, there was again the man himself. His most remarkable personality transmitted itself across the air waves in astonishing fashion. There was, too, his photographic memory. He used to say this was one of the gifts with which God had endowed him. He could take no personal credit for that, he asserted, but must just see to it that it was employed to the best advantage possible in the service of Jesus Christ and for the welfare of his fellow-men. In addition, there was his keen intellect backed up by a brilliant academic career at school and university.

One of the many outstanding characteristics of Barclay the broadcaster was his time-watching and time-keeping ability. If he was supposed to speak for x number of minutes, he could be depended upon to speak for precisely that time, no more, no less. This ability was an absolute godsend so far as programme makers were concerned.

He used to tell me that his mastery of the watch in his broadcasting was the direct result of the first broadcast he ever did. It was a "live" broadcast, a Sunday morning service, that was to occupy thirty-five minutes. William Barclay prepared everything very carefully — just as he was to do many, many times in later years — and paid particular attention, stop-watch in hand, to the timing.

He worked hard at it and had no doubt, he told me, that the service would last exactly the time specified. When the broadcast took place, everything went according to plan for the first five minutes or so. Then the producer came dashing in rather excitedly to the church from the control room to announce that a transmission fault had developed and the service had in fact not been going out on the air at all. In consequence, they had now to start all over again from the beginning. The trouble was that since it was a live broadcast and since the following programme could not be delayed, William Barclay, without notice and without time for thought, had now to compress his carefully prepared thirty-five minutes into twenty-eight.

It was this experience, traumatic though it was, that

liberated him for ever after from any fear or anxiety about time-keeping in a broadcast. On that first occasion unwelcome circumstances forced him to lay aside the paper he had so carefully prepared and so thoroughly rehearsed. It was the last situation he would ever have chosen to be in but it had happened and, as he put it to me, he just had to get on with it as best he could. His best turned out to be marvellous. He knew his material so well that the discarding of the manuscript proved to be no hindrance but rather an advantage. He said the bulk of what he had prepared to say, delivered it in a completely relaxed manner and brought the broadcast to a smooth and effective conclusion at exactly the required moment.

This set the pattern for all the vast volume of broadcasting he was to get through in subsequent years. He always prepared assiduously, always wrote his manuscript out in full, always learned it thoroughly; and always delivered the material with a combination of freedom and discipline that was his own special brand. Many a time I have been present at one of his broadcasting sessions, sometimes live, sometimes pre-recorded. His invariable practice was to deliver the opening and closing paragraphs word for word as they were written. Here every word had been carefully chosen and must be given exactly as intended. The remainder was extremely faithful to the substance of the written text but might deviate considerably in detail.

On several occasions he recorded a series of television programmes for the BBC in his own Trinity College, Glasgow. The programmes consisted of William Barclay talking for some thirty-five minutes to a studio audience on a New Testament theme and the practice was to record two programmes each evening with a break between them. It was a heavy night's work for him and I remember one occasion when the workload was even heavier than usual.

After the first of the two scheduled programmes had been completed, it was discovered that a fault had developed in the recording equipment and the programme was ruined. There was nothing else for it but that the audience should reassemble and William Barclay go through it all again.

What I found most amazing that night was not the manner in

which he accepted all this quite cheerfully as "just one of those things" but the manner in which he delivered his lecture the second time through. It was just as fluent and just as relaxed and just as compelling as the first effort; but it was by no means a verbatim reproduction. The opening and closing paragraphs were exactly as before, the written script being spoken word for word, but there were considerable differences between the first and the second runs in what came between; and yet once again the timing was precisely as desired, to the very second. That, I think, more than anything else illustrated for me what a master he was of his broadcasting craft.

Not that it was my first acquaintance with this particular facet of William Barclay's genius. Years earlier he had requested the use of my church for a radio broadcast he was to make. It was to be a live transmission from a church of a service of a "popular" character. William Barclay, of course, being a lecturer at the time did not have a church of his own; so he asked if I would make mine available to him for the broadcast and I readily did so.

He chose not to conduct the service from the pulpit and had a table and microphone set up in the chancel. I occupied the pulpit from where I conducted some preliminary devotions for my own people who were to form the congregation for the broadcast. Just before we were due to go on the air, William Barclay handed me some papers and said: "That's a copy of my script. You'd better have that so that, if anything goes wrong with me during the broadcast, you will be able to carry on."

At that time I had never done any broadcasting and the reader may well imagine, therefore, the state of near paralysis created in me by this sudden statement uttered in such matter-of-fact tones. But I tell this tale not to drawn attention to the reaction it produced in me but rather to its illumination of two very pronounced Barclay characteristics.

The first is the one I have already been discussing, his meticulous preparedness which permitted him in his broadcasting to combine a relaxed freedom of delivery with an exhaustive treatment of his subject and always to do so with exactly the timing that his producer wanted.

I sat in the pulpit that day with a copy of his script on my knee while William Barclay presented his thirty-five minute popular service. He began word for word as the script said and then I had a period of puzzled concern when I wondered if he had lost the place in that script. I began to hear paragraphs spoken in different order from what was in front of me. I began to hear the thoughts set out before me being spoken in different words from what were in the prepared text. Gradually I realised that what he was doing was to give, with little reference to his script, a very free but nevertheless remarkably accurate version of what he had written. Then, just a minute or two before the end of the address, he settled again into an exact reproduction of what was there before us both.

It was in this manner that I encountered, for the first time and somewhat dramatically, the pattern of broadcasting that I was to hear him employ so often on radio and television.

That day illustrated for me also this other notable Barclay characteristic. When he pushed those papers into my hands and said "You'd better have these, so that if anything happens to me, you can carry on," he was not trying to be over-dramatic or facetious. He meant what he said. Always for William Barclay the thing that mattered supremely was that the Lord's work should go on. Nothing mattered so much as this, that the Gospel should be communicated; and so, even if disaster or death should strike in the middle of the broadcast, his main concern was that the Word should still be preached.

His broadcasting popularity was phenomenal. First of all in the field of radio, where his unmistakable gravelly voice became a beloved institution as he spoke to all and sundry of the things of Christ and his Gospel in terms that no-one could fail to understand. As with his writing, so with all his public speaking (and private conversations, too for that matter) he had no time for language that cloaked the meaning. Words, he believed passionately, were meant to convey their user's thought in a way that could be readily grasped and understood.

This was a maxim that he followed from very early in his ministry right to the end. An incident in his first and only pastoral charge had a great influence on his use of language ever after. He had called on an elderly lady in his Renfrew congregation and she suddenly dropped into the conversation a rather wistful remark. "I'm wondering," she said, "why it is I can understand so easily everything you are saying to me just now, and yet when you are speaking from the pulpit I sometimes hardly know what you're talking about."

William Barclay went home that night to agonise long and hard over that remark. The upshot was that he resolved that, if he possibly could, he would always from then on speak in a language that even the least learned of his hearers could readily understand. He kept to that resolve to the very end of his life and millions have cause to give thanks for it.

This was true of his preaching and of his writing; but nowhere was its truth more strikingly displayed than in his phenomenal success as a broadcaster. The extremely large audiences that were attracted and held by his radio broadcasts were drawn from all walks of life; and many of these people were greatly helped by what they heard him say so plainly to them concerning Jesus Christ and his Gospel. Not a few found in his words the very key to new life.

When he finally entered the field of television broadcasting his audiences grew in number but continued to be drawn from all areas of society. His popularity and his influence increased, too; and yet it nearly was the case that he never appeared on television at all.

He liked radio and felt completely at home before a microphone whether it was in a studio or a church or anywhere else. But for years he refused all invitations to appear on television and stubbornly resisted all attempts to persuade him otherwise. He was convinced that he was not suited to this other medium and that he would not be effective on it.

I like to think that I had something to do with his being finally persuaded to "give it a go" — he used to say I had, at any rate. But it was, I think, his wife who did the trick in the end, after years of cajoling by Ronnie Falconer, BBC's head of religious broadcasting in Scotland, backed up by the persistent pleadings of friends like myself.

What a blessing it was that he was eventually persuaded to change his mind about appearing on television. He was a marvellous success from the start — and this despite the fact that many pundits tended to agree with his assessment that he was entirely the wrong formula for success on the small screen. Apart from his rasping voice and its broad Scottish accent, his style of presentation was what nearly all of the experts considered to be a sure recipe for failure.

The setting of the programme was a lecture room, with an invited audience sitting in serried rows before him. He himself simply lectured in the very same fashion as he did to his students. Using the rostrum as his base, his lecture notes carefully laid out on the lectern, he walked up and down the platform, speaking as he went, with an occasional glance at the typed script and the words pouring out in an unbroken torrent all the while.

This kind of "talking-head" presentation was considered to be the kiss of death for any religious television programme. What was more, William Barclay made it very difficult for the cameramen by virtue of his incessant movement, movement that was aggravated by his habit of fingering his hearing aid every so often. (Without his hearing aid he had been totally deaf from an early age.) The recipe seemed all wrong — and yet it produced the most delectable diet.

One series followed another for a number of years and the Barclay programmes attracted an immense following. His programme went out on Sunday nights and they were the chief talking point in most places all over the country on the Monday morning. What was perhaps most impressive and certainly what pleased William Barclay best was the vast numbers of listeners who were attracted and held from the ranks of those who never attended church.

I remember one Monday morning during one of these series. For many years I have been joining in once a week with the Motherwell Football team (my hometown team and William Barclay's, too) in their morning training session and I happened to be in the dressing room on this particular Monday morning. One of the Motherwell first team professionals — a man who was not a churchgoer — called across to me, "I saw your friend on TV last night. He is marvellous. He is the best thing I ever see on television."

Many thousands were given great enjoyment by his programmes and very many of these derived great help from them for the business of living out life day by day. If — as the experts said — the ingredients were wrong, how was it that the final product turned out so well? The answer lies in the other ingredients which some of the prognosticators failed to take sufficiently into account — things like those I have already underlined; things like William Barclay's unique ability to speak to anyone and everyone in immediately intelligible language, coupled with his vast wealth of knowledge and his willingness to spare no pains to be absolutely prepared.

The chief ingredient of success was, however, without any doubt, the man himself. Charisma of his sort is always difficult to define and it is never possible to describe it precisely or fully. But certain qualities undoubtedly contributed to his.

There was his humanity, for one. He had a broad and deep concern for his fellows. This meant that often he was an "easy touch" for someone with a hard-luck story; but he was quite prepared to be exploited a score of times rather than risk turning his back on a single opportunity of extending genuine help. This kind of compassionate outlook towards others came through in his utterances.

Another factor was that he was very down to earth. He was as much at home chatting with the car park attendant as holding conversation with the Queen or some civic or ecclesiastical dignitary. I recall going with him one day to see our beloved Motherwell team play. It was a wild and wet afternoon and it would clearly have been much more comfortable to sit in the grandstand. Left to myself I must confess that is where I would have gone. Willie, however, wanted to "be with the people" and so we stood on the exposed terracing with the majority, getting soaked just as they were but enjoying at the same time the warm-hearted camaraderie that is regularly to be found in a Scottish football crowd.

William Barclay was fond of quoting Abraham Lincoln's saying that "God must have loved the ordinary people very much for he made so many of them." The fact was that William Barclay loved them, too, and that was part of the reason that he could speak to them with such intelligibility and establish such a warm and enduring rapport with them.

This brings me to his humbleness of spirit; and this, too, surely was not only part of his personal charm but was also a contributory element in his prodigious success as a communicator. William Barclay was a very humble man and remained so even when he rose to dizzy heights of fame and popularity. He never lost sight of the fact that he too was a mortal man with faults and failings. He never grew conceited or vainglorious about his talents and achievements but maintained with sincere self-effacement that any skills he might possess were the gift of God and that therefore, any successes he might achieve were God's doing.

As a result he was always able to put himself in the other person's place and consequently never patronised anyone or any audience that he was addressing.

One mark of his humbleness was his enjoyment of stories against himself and he loved to retell them. Here is one he greatly liked. It was following one of his television series. A lady approached him in a hotel lounge and proceeded to congratulate him enthusiastically on the programmes. Then she said, "Tell me, Dr. Barclay, where is your church?" To which he replied, being at the time Professor of Divinity and Biblical Criticism at Glasgow University: "Oh, I do not have a church at the moment." "Never mind," she said, laying her hand comfortingly on his shoulder, "I am sure you will get one soon."

I can still see his shoulders heaving and his eyes twinkling as he told that tale. He enjoyed it, just as he enjoyed telling about the time he pulled in for petrol in the middle of another television series. The attendant kept staring at him and William Barclay thought to himself that here was another devoted follower summoning up the courage to speak. At last the attendant spoke up, "I've seen you on the television, haven't I?" The Professor nodded. "I knew it!" exclaimed the attendant joyfully, "You're one of those telly comedians, aren't you?"

On his retirement from his University Chair, a few of William Barclay's friends organised a public gathering in one of the Glasgow churches as a tribute to him. I was one of those friends and I was the chairman of the tribute meeting. It was a glorious and fitting occasion.

We were anxious to reflect the different aspects of Barclay the man and the servant of Christ, particularly as a communicator of the Gospel; and we attempted to do this by having a number of different people speak briefly about one side or other of him and his work. It will, I hope, highlight some features of the picture I have been trying to paint of the William Barclay I knew if I tell you just a little of what took place on an evening whose memory he prized until the day he died.

In introducing the proceedings I said that we had planned this public tribute as a kind of "everyman's thank you" to William Barclay and so the speakers had been chosen to represent those masses of people from all walks of life who were, as I expressed it, "debtors in the faith" to him.

We began with the Rev. Bob Brown, one of his former students now in his first ministerial charge. He thanked the professor not only for what he had taught his students but even more for his interest in them as individuals and for his willingness to give his time and his wisdom so generously in order to help and advise whenever help and advice were sought. "We knew that you were always very busy and were probably in fact engaged at any given time in writing three books, two lectures and a speech; but you always gave us your undivided attention with no hint of hurrying us, as if the only thing that mattered at that moment was what we might have to say to you. I and all your former students thank you tonight because you communicated the Gospel to us not only by what you said but even more by what you were. We loved you for it then and we love you for it now."

Bobby Watson, captain of Motherwell Football Club first eleven, said that his tribute represented the gratitude of the players and spectators of the sporting world of Scotland. Archie Maynard, shipyard worker and now an elder of William Barclay's former charge in Renfrew, spoke of his tremendous impact at that time upon the youth of that church and town of whom he himself then was one. Ian Chapman of Collins the Publishers spoke of his ministry in print; Ronnie Falconer spoke of his broadcasting ministry; David Wylie, a Glasgow elder, spoke particularly of the gratitude of the people of his own city.

The Rev. Bob Martin from Princeton, New Jersey, flew across from California to speak on behalf of the scores of thousands in the U.S.A. who were Barclay admirers and beneficiaries. The Rev. Colin Campbell, William Barclay's own parish minister, paid tribute to his wife, Katherine, as well as to the guest of honour himself, and the Rev. Stanley Munro, lifelong friend since college days, made a speech of sincere acclamation as he handed over a cheque that represented the gifts of grateful men and women from all over the world, a cheque which the recipient used to found the "Barclay Lectureship in Communication of the Christian Gospel".

The pinnacle of the evening was reached with William Barclay's reply. It was vintage Barclay — humble and grateful, brilliant and moving. In typical fashion he had us, in the one moment, rocking with laughter and, in the next, deeply moved, at times having almost the feeling that in a second or two we would actually see the New Jerusalem before our eyes. The main theme of his speech was that of thankfulness — to his parents; to his schooling; to his students; to his friends; to his wife and family; and especially "to God who has been so astonishingly good to me all the days of my life".

It was right and fitting, I thought, that this same note of joyful gratitude should be dominant in his funeral service, despite the sorrow that was also inevitably present. Even the weather put on mourning garb that day. It was a bleak Scottish winter's day with snow lying on the ground and sleet slanting incessantly down from a lowering sky. The fact that the whole world seemed to be in mourning for William Barclay was typified for me by the fact that I noticed a policewoman directing the funeral traffic quietly weeping as she went about her task.

It was with heaviness of heart that we gathered, hundreds of us, into the church standing in the crematorium grounds for the service that was to be conducted by Willie's own minister and personal friend for many years, Colin Campbell. But the atmosphere of the service was mainly one of triumph. This was exactly right and exactly as William Barclay would have wanted it, granted that there was a funeral service at all.

He often used to declare in his gruff, authoritative tones that he would prefer that there was no funeral service for him when he died. This was one of many topics of friendly argument he had with his friends. He was of course, an inveterate coat-trailer, especially on more private occasions. He liked nothing better than to stir it up occasionally in conversation. On this matter however, he was, I believe, more than half in earnest. We used to try to repel this suggestion with as much force as we could muster; but he would persist with the unyielding obstinacy he so often summoned to his side when in his heart of hearts he knew that he was continuing the argument mainly for argument's sake.

"Funeral services," he would say, "are an unnecessary fuss and an unnecessary cause of additional grief. They are superfluous so far as Christians are concerned, for the Christian knows better than anyone else that the body has done its work and is no longer of any importance. It should just be disposed of as quietly as possible — the real person no longer has any part in it. In any case," he would go on, "funerals are often an occasion for fulsome and insincere tributes being paid to the departed; and I do not want flowery and flattering eulogies spoken of me when I depart."

We used to try to point out to him that this was a selfish attitude. Of course the Christian knows that his body is of no consequence after death; but surely, we would say, you must allow your many friends the opportunity to pay their respects to you, as they will certainly want to do.

In the event his funeral service was the kind of simple and sincere thing of which he would, I am sure, have approved. We sang a Scottish metrical psalm and we sang one of his most favourite hymns, "My Times are in Thy Hand". The minister read some of the triumphant Scriptures that proclaim so gloriously the Christian assurance of the life everlasting; and he led us in a prayer of thanksgiving for the life and work of William Barclay that was magnificently moving.

That prayer I felt was just right for the occasion and just right for William Barclay's memory. I feel sure that it was a prayer that William Barclay would have been humbly pleased to acknowledge; and yet the odd thing is that it was not at all a prayer that he could or would have written himself.

William Barclay never used the traditional "thee" and "thou" when addressing the Almighty in prayer. For all the time I had known him he had firmly believed in setting aside that kind of language in public worship as being a hindrance rather than a help in the endeavour to lead men and women into the presence of God.

Colin Campbell's prayer was couched in the more traditional style of "thee" and "thou" still favoured by the majority of Scottish ministers. He and William Barclay had been friends for many years even before the cross-currents of life decreed that Colin should become Willie's minister; and the fact that Colin persisted with prayer language of which Willie so thoroughly disapproved did not diminish that friendship in the slightest. This was just another measure of the true Christian character of William Barclay. He did not fall out with any man or take offence at him because he disagreed with him about this or that.

It is the sad fact that it did not always work like that the other way round. William Barclay was subjected to many an unkindness and to many a hurt simply because someone disagreed with him in his understanding of some aspect of the faith they held in common. Many a time for instance, he has shown me a letter — perhaps following a broadcast — which attacked him quite viciously for some supposed heresy or the like; and in all probability the letter would be signed "Yours in the Master's service" or in similar fashion.

One of the most shocking instances of this kind of thing — and the one which wounded him most cruelly — came to him after a radio broadcast. He was giving a series of short morning talks on the miracles of Jesus. One morning he spoke about the stilling of the storm. He said that he could not tell what exactly took place on the Sea of Galilee on that long ago occasion, but he did know that Jesus had then stilled the storm of fear that was raging in the disciples' hearts. He went on to say that the most important thing this story had to tell us today was not what physical events occurred on Lake Galilee twenty centuries ago, but that we could be sure that Jesus was able to still any storm in our hearts today. He said, too, how thankful he was that he had found this proved true in his own experience. When his daughter Barbara was accidentally drowned at the age of nineteen, Jesus had stilled the storm of grief and sorrow in his heart and given him the strength and the courage to go on.

A few days later, obviously much grieved, he showed me a letter which he had just received. The writer upbraided him for what he alleged was a heretical treatment of the miracle and continued, "I am now able to see why God killed your daughter, lest you should corrupt her any more with your heresy."

William Barclay, for his part, returned good for evil when anyone attacked him for his views: and consistently replied to unfair criticism or even abuse with graciousness and charity. When The Upper Room conferred their citation on him (along with James S. Stewart) in 1975 in the Assembly Rooms in Edinburgh, some followers of Pastor Jack Glass picketed the location with placards proclaiming such ludicrous slogans as "Barclay is a heretic" and "Barclay the enemy of the Gospel".

I for my part was both saddened and angered by such slanders against the name of a man who, in my opinion, and that of many others, had done more than anyone else in his generation to commend and promote the Gospel of his Saviour. I engaged in some sharp but quite fruitless argument with some of the pickets. William Barclay on the other hand went across with outstretched hand to Pastor Glass and said, "Let's shake hands, Jack, and agree to differ amicably. After all, we're both on Christ's side." That kind of graciousness was typical of him.

It was fitting that we should sing his favourite hymn at his funeral service. He particularly liked the words of the third verse:

> My times are in Thy hand,
> Why should I doubt or fear?
> My Father's hand will never cause
> His child a needless tear.

To those of us gathered in that church for William Barclay's funeral, the last verse seemed particularly appropriate:

> My times are in Thy hand:
> I'll always trust in Thee:
> And, after death, at Thy right hand
> I shall for ever be.

It was appropriate because William Barclay had often sung these words himself and they joyfully expressed his steadfast faith in the life to come.

I want to put that on record before I bring these reflections on William Barclay to a close. His belief in the life everlasting was real and strong. I was both surprised and shocked to read in one of the newspaper obituaries of him that "William Barclay had severe doubts about the life hereafter".

That was simply not true. He had serious and penetrating doubts about the ideas some people held about the nature of the life of heaven; but he had no doubts whatsoever that beyond this life Jesus had in store for his people something even better and richer. I often heard him affirm strongly and unambiguously his belief in the life to come and you will find the same affirmation many times in his writings.

I remember particularly, after Barbara's death, his saying to me that he had never been more sure of the life to come than then; and he never wavered from that firm conviction.

That is why I do not think of William Barclay as merely dead. Oh, I miss him very much; but, like the millions of others who have cause to give thanks for him, whether or not they ever knew him personally, I rejoice that he is now more gloriously alive than ever before.

William Barclay was a big man in every way. He was glad to be alive and he enjoyed life immensely, finding its gladness and its satisfaction all the deeper because he knew Jesus as his Saviour and Lord. It is a great loss to all the world that he has gone from amongst us and that is a source of acute sadness to all who knew him personally or through his utterances, spoken or written. At the same time, we may be glad that he is still vibrantly alive. We are much the poorer for his passing but heaven is that much the richer. Not only so. His influence upon the world and its people will last, I believe, as long as time endures.

5 – Barclay among the scholars
by Johnston R. McKay

Johnston McKay, a Glasgow and Cambridge graduate, is minister of Paisley Abbey and a regular religious broadcaster. He has also been assistant at St. Giles' Cathedral in Edinburgh and had his first full ministry in Glasgow close to the Rangers football ground at Ibrox. He was joint editor of a volume of theological studies presented to Barclay on his retirement from Glasgow University.

The evening of Willie Barclay's funeral, I sat with Douglas Aitken, Senior Radio Producer of the Religious Department of BBC (Scotland), preparing a radio tribute which was to be broadcast the following Sunday evening. Douglas had arranged, at obviously very short notice, contributions to the programme from all five continents, but so far none of the contributors represented the world of British New Testament scholarship. I suggested a former teacher of mine, a good friend, John O'Neill of Westminster College, Cambridge, and so we telephoned him.

"John, you'll have heard that Willie Barclay has died. Would you be prepared to go into a studio in London on Sunday afternoon and talk to me about his contribution to New Testament scholarship?"

"Ye-es," came the reply after a moment or two, and I sensed that the hesitation in his voice wasn't entirely due to John's Australian drawl. I suddenly became afraid that the academic in John O'Neill might prove as snobbishly critical of the popular scholar as so many others had been. It was after all, a Cambridge New Testament teacher who once dismissed Willie Barclay as "the man who just tells you what Jesus had for breakfast". But the invitation had been extended, and so details were confirmed for the following Sunday afternoon.

"What was Willie Barclay's contribution to New Testament scholarship?" I asked, a little nervously, when the interview began.

"Johnston, if you had asked me that question a week ago, I wouldn't have known what to say. But since Willie Barclay's death, I've been reading his books again, and my admiration for him grows and grows as I've read these pages. The trouble with New Testament scholars is that we're always stopping people from reading the New Testament. We are always pulling them up, and saying that there are difficulties, whereas Willie would take on the problem. He poured out what he knew about the Roman world and the Greek world, what he knew about the customs of New Testament times, and by building up detail, encourage you to take on the whole of the New Testament. Really, I feel I have come here to do penance for New Testament scholars, because I am afraid we didn't realise that he was telling us we were on the wrong track; that we had been stopping people from reading the Bible whereas his whole aim was to encourage them to read the Bible."

The tape had been running, and we broadcast it. In the radio programme which I am still most proud to have taken part in, that was the most remarkable thing said. For academics did tend to dismiss Willie Barclay as a lightweight. They thought of him, sometimes, with only thinly veiled contempt, as a "mere populariser". When he applied for the Chair of Divinity and Biblical Criticism at Glasgow University (having failed in at least one attempt to obtain a Chair elsewhere) his fiercest critic on the appointing committee expressed the view that no-one deserving respect as a scholar should have his books read by so many people!

All his days, Willie Barclay suffered from a form of academic inferiority complex. Sometimes it seemed as if this stemmed from the attitude his colleagues took towards him. Often, and quite absurdly, it appeared to result from an exaggerated respect for academic institutions which he had never attended. Oxford and Cambridge he held in a quite irrational respect, although in his latter years he spent much of each summer at Mansfield College, Oxford, perhaps savouring a little of the world he envied others their participation in. John O'Neill remembers that when Willie Barclay discovered that he had studied in Germany, he became almost deferential in his attitude to the younger man.

It is difficult to explain why a man who had such a success as a preacher and communicator, to whom international fame and public honour came, and rested so lightly on his ample shoulders, should have had such an element of self-doubt and self-questioning in his make-up. Maybe a psychologist could have offered an explanation. His friends certainly had one: it was the man's modesty.

Some scholars easily accept the kind of acclaim which Barclay received, and readily grow to regard it as simply their rightful due. That was never the case with Willie Barclay. He belonged to the group of scholars whose scholarship makes them more aware of their own limitations than confidently assured of their superiority. In this he had something in common with another great New Testament scholar of an earlier age, R. H. Lightfoot, who had to be forced by his friends to apply for a Chair at Oxford which he himself felt unfit to occupy — because he did not possess a first-class degree. Willie Barclay did gain a first-class degree, in classics, but he once wrote: "I have an essentially second-class mind. In all the books I have written I have explained and expounded other men's ideas. It is the simple truth that I never had an original idea in my life." Doubtless so. But Willie Barclay made the ideas and the theories, the words and the concepts which he borrowed from others, much more exciting, interesting and compelling than their supposedly sole begetters did. And in many cases, that took real originality!

Willie Barclay's modesty was more than a personal characteristic. It influenced how he taught. His sort of modesty could, in a sense, be regarded as a mixed blessing in a teacher. He was always willing to listen to new students, and to others in the academic world, whose detailed knowledge of the New Testament in no way matched his own. He was always ready to concede that a student had a point of view worth respecting, and of course that is a fine quality in a teacher. Sometimes, however, one had the impression that Willie Barclay was not just willing to listen but almost unwilling to criticise, when his criticism would have been founded on information and research of which others had no real knowledge. He was notoriously unable to hurt or offend people, but, it has to be said, sometimes he did manage to hurt because he was unable at an early stage to be critical. There were students whom he encouraged to believe had ability they did not, in the event, prove to possess. Willie could not bear to tell them so until too late. Kindness is a great human virtue, and Willie Barclay had it to excess. Occasionally that innate kindliness over-ruled his better judgment.

It was not just his kindliness which made him accord to the views of students and others a respect they did not, perhaps, deserve. It was, again, this modesty about his own capabilities. He was, undoubtedly, a great scholar in the field of New Testament words and the New Testament background. Words were his stock-in-trade: not just the words with which he communicated the Christian Gospel so effectively, but the words in which that Gospel was first committed to print. He had an encyclopaedic knowledge of New Testament language and classical literature. No need for him to feed the Epistles of St. Paul or the writings of Herodotus into a computer to find out how often and in which contexts various words were used. His quite phenomenal memory for almost everything he had ever read retained such information. He was not, however, a great theologian, either as a student of what is loosely called "the theology of the New Testament", or in a personally creative sense. He had his limitations as an interpreter of the New Testament. They were, however, the limitations which prove the strengths of a great preacher, who see texts, passages and themes in terms of their communicability, rather than as ideas in isolation, to be examined for their own sake.

"Faith seeking understanding" is a classic definition of theology. I am not sure that Willie Barclay's faith ever required him to pursue the understanding of it, and perhaps that is why he did not rank in the front line of theologians. David L. Edwards, Barclay's publisher for many years with the S.C.M. Press, once described Willie Barclay's faith as "Liberal Protestantism: the Fatherhood of God, the brotherhood of man, the power of love and truth — and not much else that is absolutely essential in understanding the message of Jesus." It was, I believe, a very accurate description, but it described, in Willie Barclay's case, a faith which contained all the elements requiring understanding. He regarded his role as one of providing the facts, the background, and the explanations which made faith reasonable, and, more importantly, intelligible. He would not have pursued the task of the explorative theologian, as, for instance, did a colleague of his in the Glasgow Divinity Faculty, Ronald Gregor Smith.

Willie Barclay seems to have been totally convinced that if you illustrated (as he did with consummate skill) what the New Testament was saying, and if you explained more clearly its terms and concepts, then you had made the faith more reasonable. And, of course, that is precisely where his strength as a communicator and a preacher lay, allied to that intensely human personality which immediately attracted attention. A theologian, however, must have the kind of mind which needs to probe beyond the illustrative.

In that respect, Willie Barclay's admission that he did not have an original mind is probably an accurate admission. Probably he never accepted that the number of scholars who made genuinely original contributions to their chosen field is very limited indeed. That is as true of theology as it is of any other subject. So, in the realm of theology, minutiae is the order of the day. More and more is being learned and discovered of less and less. Willie Barclay could have made an international reputation in a narrowing scholarly field of New Testament language — his astounding knowledge of classical and New Testament Greek would have assured that. But his personality, and his burning urge to communicate, would never have been satisfied with the sort of scholarly interchange which is carried on in learned journals and academic gatherings. Because he chose another sphere, the academic estimate of him was less high. That, however, was true of another person who was dismissed because he did not cite the learned authorities and quote the respected sources. But the common people heard him gladly. In a way, if Willie Barclay had taught in the Scotland of a previous generation, his outlook would have been unexceptionable. Scholars of the calibre of James Denney, James Moffatt, and George Adam Smith did not imagine that they compromised their academic reputation by writing and preaching for the popular world.

Willie Barclay never ceased saying that he wrote for and preached to "the plain man" (who was mentioned in the titles of so many of his books). In this he succeeded to an extent that nobody else has, nor could anyone else come near to emulating him.

When Willie Barclay retired, along with James Miller I edited a book of essays in his honour. At the outset of the project, Willie himself was adamant that we must seek contributions from other scholars, but they had to be written "for the plain man". We knew it was a fruitless attempt, and in time he came to accept that it was. Other scholars just could not communicate as he did with those who did not have a scholarly interest or an academic background. He was unique, or, as one plain man put it in plain man's language: "He was magic!"

6 – Barclay's Biblicality: mode and method
by Clive Rawlins

Clive Rawlins, a former publishing manager of the Saint Andrew Press, was ordained to the ministry of the Baptist Church in England and later moved to the United Reformed Church. He is the editor and compiler of the index to the revised edition of the Barclay Daily Study Bible *and also edited* Men and Affairs, *the book of Barclay's long-running review page in the* Expository Times.

In just over twenty-five years, William Barclay wrote more than seventy books.[1] His name is known world-wide and is associated with a style of Christian writing which is simple, direct, devotional, not free from controversy, and yet — above all — Biblical in its orientation. During those years he was usually top of the religious best-seller lists, or very near to it, which earned him, among other epithets, the reputation of being "a battery-hen of Biblical commentators"!

Yet despite this prodigious output, his name is not coupled with any particular piece of theological work; he has not produced a contribution or a theory which will be remembered in the academic halls of fame. Indeed, his name does not even feature in many of the most prominent books of Biblical introduction, and his books are only infrequently mentioned on reading lists in our colleges or universities. By and large the world of scholarship has passed him by.

Why should this be? How is it that a man with such a prolific writing record, following a highly successful university education in Scotland and Germany, and the one-time incumbent of one of the prestigious theological chairs, could leave so little trace of his activities in his subject's literature?

There is more than one possible answer, but if it be true that the world of scholarship passed him by it is no less true that he, likewise, passed it by. Not in the sense that he was unaware of what was being done or written, but in the sense that he had other interests at stake; he was never a pure researcher, interested in knowledge merely for its own sake. He lived and worked, despite his university base, not in any ivory tower, but in the flux of human experience and endeavour. In one of his journalistic pieces, later, as was his usual practice, to be incorporated into a book,[2] he enjoins his readers to ask the fundamental question, "What is the point of what I'm doing?" Typically, he illustrates one possible answer from his own world of scholarship, and so speaks of the many books "which have undoubtedly taken years of research, and which, regarded as pure scholarship, are monuments of erudition, *but what's the point of them?*"

He challenges his readers with a quotation:

> Epictetus used to say, "Vain is the discourse of philosophy by which no human heart is healed." It is an interesting test — and, if it were applied, quite a number of erudite works would emerge as vanity.

This is not the way to earn scholarly approval! But it is very typical and, indeed, central to his whole life and work. He was essentially a theological or, more accurately, a religious pragmatist; a man caught up with — and perhaps at times engulfed by — the human situation, in all its aspects. If at times he manifested a prophetic perception and tone, it was only because at the heart of the man rested a priestly empathy: one which was able to deal gently with men, being surrounded itself by the same temptations, and understanding well their ever-so-human problems and failings.

This does not mean that he was not a theological thinker. He was, but the ground-base of his thinking and the parameters within which he worked were thoroughly Biblical, as we shall see. His thinking was not philosophical, but practical. "I think in pictures," he was to remark in his autobiography.[3] He was somewhat impatient of research *qua* research; of scholarship purely for its own sake. He believed that life was for living, and that the Bible was for introducing to that life that vitality which really was life. He did not seek merely to describe the symptoms of man's plight as that of a specimen or sample, still less to meddle with a simple prognosis; he went straight to the heart of the matter and sought to apply the healing by making much of the cure.

His attitude towards scholarship, therefore, may best be given in his own words, in the general introduction to his *Daily Study Bible*, his *magnum opus*.[4] He writes that the series has always had one aim, "to convey the results of scholarship to the ordinary reader".[5] William Barclay, as we have seen, was essentially a man of the people; he knew and understood and loved the ordinary man; he wrote for him, and it was fitting that one of his best known series of books was named after "the plain man". He had an immense and warm human sympathy, which continuously earthed the high voltage of his scholarship and learning. Like A. S. Peake before him, William Barclay had "a genius for friendship",[6] which made itself felt through his books and thus reached out beyond his desk around the world, and involved him in a pastoral ministry which was literally world-wide.

The comparison with A. S. Peake is highly significant. "No-one," Barclay wrote in reviewing John T. Wilkinson's excellent biography, "did more for me and my generation."[7] and he added that Peake "delighted in the saying that he was a 'theological middleman' and I should be happy if the same could be said of me." This popularising was no self-indulgence on Peake's part, still less on Barclay's, but serious business: the conscious interpretation of their life's work. As Peake was to say in his commentary, by which his name is still rightly venerated today, "it is an editor's special duty, as 'occupying the place of the unlearned', to keep constantly in mind [the needs of non-technical folk — Barclay's plain man]."[8] Elsewhere Peake commented, "I felt the immense importance of this class of work and the duty which scholars owed to the Church and people in general."[9] Further, he noted that, "it is as great a service to bring the common opinion of scholars to clear expression as to increase by one more the number of venturesome hypotheses." This was a consistent view of his, and even found expression in his inaugural lecture at the founding of the University of Manchester's Faculty of Theology. He writes[10] that "a university sinks below the level of its privilege and duty unless it hears the call to share the gains of scholarship with those whose life runs in other grooves."

He cites[11] with warm approbation the words of Harnack, that great New Testament scholar and Church historian:

> The theologians of every country only half discharge their duties if they think it enough to treat of the Gospels in their recondite language of learning and bury it in scholarly folios.

Twenty-five years later, on the anniversary of the founding of that same chair of Peake's which had regrettably been vacated just recently by his untimely death, F. C. Burkitt was to remark,[12]

> It is most important, in my opinion, that the specialists retain a vivid sympathy and interest in their subject as it appeals to the average man, to the general public . . . There is a danger lest the discoveries of scientific learning become the property of a coterie, without real influence on the thought of mankind in general.

Burkitt pointed out how much more specialised scholarship had become since Peake had first set out his principle of popularisation. How much more is that true of our own day, and therefore of Barclay's work!

The specialists' views — the views held by plain men and women. Such are the polarities Barclay sought to unite, regarding his writing and his broadcasting as "the most important thing I have done"[13] and says, in summing it all up, "If I were to begin life over again, I would choose exactly the same service." Service it was, the hidden service of countless, self-denying hours of solitary vigil; and popularisation was its name.

But popularisation is not "vulgarisation". H. G. Wells sought to ridicule James Henry by saying, "I'm not an author. I'm a publicist. My work is just high-class journalism."[14] Barclay never claimed much about his own work; indeed, he sought to minimise it by understatement, and frequently ignored it even when citing it would have been in his readers' best interests. We have already seen[15] that he could actually forget about the first book he wrote, and I am told that he never re-read any of his books, once published. But popularising *was* serious business: he was making something widely known, not making it cheap. Like Peake before him, he was not seeking to disseminate some sort of religious populism, still less spiritual pap. "A superficial skating over of a doctrine will not do,"[16] he said bluntly. He was engaged in, not a propagandist's dogmatism, but what W. E. Sangster called "the battle for intelligibility".

Barclay's writing is remarkably lucid, flowing and forceful, replete with comments and illustrations which are both apposite and telling. But his objectives were somewhat different from Peake's, as were his means. Peake definitely sought to popularise *scholars' views*: Barclay much less so. Peake was more interested in the exegetical aspect of his work than Barclay, and found greater space for critical problems. Barclay was essentially an expositor, and found opportunity to express, sometimes at great length, the homiletical aspect. This damaged his work at times, and made it unbalanced. (For example, the treatment he gives his text in the *Daily Study Bible* is unequal, and the revised edition has not sought to rectify this. One only has to compare his commentary on Acts — to be strictly fair, he does not call that series of books "commentaries" — with, say, Revelation, to see that this is so.)

At times he will expend himself on brilliant illustration of secondary aspects and leave altogether untouched vital areas of the text. (An example of this is given below regarding 2 Timothy 3:16 and *theopneustos*.) At times he wrote devotional material *simpliciter*, and thus left large subjects and problems without comment. Peake, too, could do this, but the volumes of output are different and Barclay's sheer scale of activity accentuates this aspect, especially as he tended to duplicate points already made adequately.

There was another difference between the two men: Barclay often wrote for a younger constituency than Peake, who was consumed by the need for worker-education, which was then the rage and was so well fulfilled by the work of the Workers' Educational Association (for which Manchester was a notable centre). Barclay's readers were very often young people, for he took great pleasure in his involvement with the Boys' Brigade and the YMCA; he also wrote for the young people's department of the Church of Scotland. Even today his books are still being introduced into training courses for these and similar groups, and with the growth of the Church in Third World countries they are being used more and more widely.

To a very large extent this popularising work grew because it was thrust on him, not because he sought it. He mentions that he never wrote a book except by invitation.[17] This aspect is not sufficiently taken into account, but it was crucial to his whole manner and range of working. Perhaps he was not sufficiently critical of it; perhaps he accepted invitations too easily; certainly he allowed the re-publication of his works too readily, as the *Daily Study Bible* revision shows. One thing, however, is absolutely true: they met a need, and meet it still. The world needs popularisers and William Barclay has been found to do the job, and to do it effectively, across many cultures and within many denominational structures and attitudes. Like Peake before him, he was the man for the job.

Many of these books were the results of his journalistic enterprises. Even *The First Three Gospels*, which comes nearest to being an academic work among his Biblical writings, began in this way. He could write to order, and was therefore the ideal person to trust to a regular slot in such periodicals as the *British Weekly* and the *Expository Times.* Peake had likewise refused to turn up his nose at this form of journalism, and had provided most valuable leadership to his denomination through it.

In all this, the "battle for intelligibility" was foremost. He sought to write of a full Christian understanding of God and the world, as he understood it, without watering it down or blunting its challenge. This is necessarily bound up with a certain honesty of thought, and language, and purpose. He wrote:[18]

> Superficial talking can neither comfort the heart nor satisfy the mind . . . Sheer honesty, even if it was an honesty of a fight for faith not yet victorious, was far more

effective than a bland and superficial orthodoxy. Nothing can be a substitute for the accent of honesty.

It was an honesty which was to be marvellously liberating for not a few of those "plain men and women" for whom he wrote; and was to earn him sharp, and at times wounding, vilification from those whose minds were hermetically sealed against the expression of doctrine in anything other than credal (as opposed to Biblical) form and language.

It is fair to say that he was not always consistent in the working out of his thinking, and at times his theology displayed some odd gaps and leaps of reason; at times it threatened to be somewhat self-contradictory, and he enjoyed trailing his coat. A lover of the classics, there was a real element of the Socratic gadfly about him. And why not? He was affronted by the closed mind, and could express himself forcefully on it: "The history of progress" (he comments on *Matthew* 9:16,[19] which he significantly entitles "The problem of the new idea") is the "history of the overcoming of the prejudices of the shut mind".

He castigates with near-prophetic fury those whose minds are culpably closed: "The word 'disciple' means *a learner . . .* The shut mind cannot serve (Christ)!"[20] And, "There can be no religion without adventure . . . God can find no use for the shut mind."[21] And finally: "When a man's mind becomes so shut that it can accept no new truth, he is mentally and spiritually dead."[22]

Understanding, open-mindedness, sheer intellectual honesty governed Barclay's interpretive approach to the scriptures and to doctrine (in that order!); the desire to learn and to know was basic and all-pervading. For this reason he could write: "The church which has no Bible Class is a church in whose work an essential element is missing."[23]

But faith did not come easily to him, despite his self-description as "a natural believer". (Here is one of those self-contradictions to which I referred earlier). Notwithstanding a natural willingness to believe, a pre-disposition even, he could talk freely about "the mental sweat of rethinking things"[24] in a way which reveals the painful processes he himself pursued. He was well aware that

. . . a faith that can be neatly stated in a series of prop-
ositions and neatly proved in a series of logical steps like a
geometric theorem is a contradiction in terms.[25]

He concludes by quoting Tertullian's ridiculous comment,
born of experience, "I believe because it is impossible."

This struggle for faith, this readiness to discount what he
most firmly wished to commit himself to, did not just arise out
of his extraordinarily wide reading (in the classics, in historical
and critical works, in biography and in fiction — was there
recently any other theologian who devoured so much literature and wrote so prolifically?). At the heart of his thinking
there was a hurt, a hurt from which we all share as partici-
pators in "the human condition", but which Barclay was
forced to grapple with enduringly through the sheer sensitivity
of his mind and spirit. It was first brought home to him in the
death of his beautiful and much-loved mother, after a painful
ignobling illness. "You'll have a new note in your preaching
now," his father had drily commented:[26] a remark he could
not forget. It was even more deeply engraved upon him in the
tragic death of his daughter in a yachting accident. His beliefs
were formed from this sort of brutal encounter with reality,
and whilst without philosophy or system,[27] he sought to build
them into a coherent view of God and the world. At all times
his thinking was sharpened and antagonised by the Biblical
record. Moreover, his pastoral care of his people at Renfrew
during thirteen years, and his concern at the plight of some of
his fellow-citizens of Glasgow for many more, added to which
were wide travelling and a large pastoral correspondence, all
isolated and honed the problems of faith for today.

To William Barclay understanding and communicating the
Christian faith — *the good news*, as he was wont to remind his
readers — was more important than systematic knowledge
and the experiential knowledge of Jesus far more important
than that harnessed within a "correct" academic framework.
He quotes approvingly the words of Cromwell to his troops,
"We speak *things*",[28] and adds; "He meant that he was not
dealing with abstract ideas, but with concrete realities."
Barclay was immersed in the rush of human experience: he did
not delay to refine his thinking but delivered a word of help

and succour. He was driven to do so, for whether by direct contact with the public through his preaching or broadcasting, or indirectly with them via his published articles and books, or in training men for the ministry (like Peake he saw his university post primarily as a means to that end), he must make known his message and his experience: he must communicate; there could be no knowledge "for its own sake". He expressed it in this way in his Laird Lectures:

> Here is the reason for the study of the New Testament, not that we should know the history or the linguistics or anything else, but that we should know him of whom it tells; for we can never communicate Jesus Christ to others, until we know him ourselves.

We shall see later that this is the centrepoint of Barclay's theology and, indeed, of his world-view: Jesus; the *historical* Jesus. "The life of Jesus in Palestine and his death under Pontius Pilate are beyond argument."[29] — Such was the decisiveness of his commitment to this central *motif* in his work. And in another place he wrote, "For me Jesus is the centre and the soul of the whole matter."[30] We might put it this way:

> What is Professor Barclay seeking to popularise? — The message of Jesus (which, in his view *is* Jesus himself).
> And what is the basis of that message? — The Biblical record.

That is the simple reason why William Barclay became a minister, why he accepted a university lectureship, why be became Professor of Divinity and Biblical Criticism, and why he wrote more than seventy books. His relationship with Jesus Christ was the adequate *raison d'être* for all that he wrote or said. That relationship, and the knowledge was which ensued from it, was Biblical through and through.

The matter has been put very finely by the editors of the volume which was presented to him on his retirement from his chair. (Notably, these editors were parish ministers, not fellow academics). In their preface[31] they draw our attention exclusively to his

> deep awareness of the Biblicality of all things and all subjects. Historical and social issues, scientific and ethical problems, current crises and future hopes, William Barclay brings all these into a sharp focus under a Biblical lens. This Biblicality, the viewing of all things from and the bringing of issues to a Biblical vision, characterises the life and work of William Barclay.

Ronald Falconer illustrated the same point when he revealed[32] that Barclay's main preparation for his Baird Lectures (on Christian Ethics) was

> to read the whole of the New Testament afresh, and most of the Old Testament too, in order to come to a scriptural understanding of the Christian Ethic, not only in the personal and sexual field but in the industrial and international areas as well.

Barclay was a man of the Book; not slavishly, nor blindly, but carefully testing, again and again, his whole approach and tenets by its teaching, purpose and goal. Let us look at four areas of his Biblical understanding.

1. His doctrine of scripture: the Bible as word of God.
2. Its pivotal point: Jesus, the Word of God.
3. The doctrine of inspiration: a dual activity between God and man.
4. His rules of interpretation: a contemporary hermeneutic.

I: The Bible as word of God

Despite many comments to the contrary by his detractors, this was of fundamental importance to him; an article of faith which, though open to challenge, was never reduced or weakened by him. His Biblicality is crucial precisely because he owned the Bible as God's word. "We begin," he roundly declares in his most useful book, *Introducing the Bible*,[33] "with the assumption of Arminius that 'the Church is that community which recognises the word of God in the scriptures'." He had stated earlier[34] that "in all the controversies of religion the scriptures are the final court of appeal". And further, that it (the Bible) "is still for the Christian the supreme rule of faith and life".

He never moved from this basic affirmation. It is here that we see Barclay at his most presbyterian. He seldom argues *for* the Bible's position as word of God: it is there, given, available to be tried and tested by experience. History has proved it, not only by its very power to exist against all the machinations of men to destroy it, but in the way it has transformed life and society whenever given a chance to do so. Nothing, he was firmly persuaded, could bind or weaken the word of God:

> As we study the history of the Bible, and as we come to see how it came to be what it is today, we see God speaking to men in every age and generation through men whom his Spirit inspired, and through events through which he was making his will known to man. We see the word of God establishing itself in the hearts and minds of men . . .[35]

Of its power to bring men to an understanding of God and his will he bluntly writes[36] that "In simple fairness, no man seeking for the truth has any right to neglect the reading of the Bible. A book with a record such as it has cannot be disregarded."

No scholar this century has talked so publicly and written so prolifically as William Barclay has on the scriptures, but we should note how they *silence* him, as he puts himself under their teaching and authority:

> When we study the Bible we should be very sure that we are listening to God and not the echo of our own voice.[37]

It is this willingness to listen, to still his tongue and arrest his pen, which explains his continual freshness in exposition and application; as of one taught, under authority. He has a dynamic awareness of its own inherent life and activity: "The word of God is instinct with life" is his forceful translation of *Hebrews* 4:12, adding that "it is a living issue for all men of all times . . . it is something that every man must face."[38]

The Bible's power and ability to speak meaningfully to our own day is part of his recognition of it as the word of God. "Anything," he writes, "which makes the New Testament other than contemporary mistranslates it."[39] Thus, whilst delighting in the *Authorised Version*'s beauty, he had no hesitation in recommending a modern version, and underlined the seriousness of his recommendation by himself translating the New Testament twice.

At times this insistency on the Bible's contemporaneity threatens his own stress on its historicity (another of the Barclay self-contradictions). A good example is found in his treatment of the miracles of Jesus:[40]

> The miracles of Jesus in the New Testament are meaningful; everyone of them tells us something about God . . . First, I try to explain the miracles, not to explain them away. The purpose of the explanation is to enable the reader to appropiate the wonder-working power of Jesus himself. The second aim is to present Jesus as someone, not who *did* things, but who *does* things. The greatest danger in Christianity is to think of Jesus as someone who is to be remembered. He is someone to be experienced and met.

The Bible is the word of God because it has proved itself to be so in the experience of men, because it proves itself in our experience today: that was Barclay's essential viewpoint and affirmation.

II: Jesus the Word of God

It is central to Barclay's whole standing and commitment that the pivotal point of the Biblical literature is Jesus, himself the Word of God.

Few New Testament expositors have been at such pains to explain and emphasise this awareness. It is writ large throughout his publications and acts as the standard for testing theological validity, whatever its source: "It is our duty to use our minds and set them adventuring: but the test must ever be agreement with the teaching of Jesus Christ as the scriptures present it to us."[41]

He puts this aspect even more graphically when he claims that the Bible is only properly understood when it is understood christologically:[42]

> The Old Testament foretells Christ; the Gospels tell of Jesus the Christ; and the apostles bring the message of Jesus to men.

Such comment was bound to bring a rejoinder from the academic that it was to over-simplify the matter. Barclay knew it did, and knew the criticism would be voiced. But it did not prevent him from saying it, and repeating it, and making is as plain as he knew how: this was his central, pivotal affirmation; what he most surely believed. For this reason the subject has high importance in his autobiography, in which he says[43]

> For me the most important single text in the Bible is *John* 1:14, "and the Word became flesh and dwelt among us." . . . the supreme truth of Christianity is that in Jesus I see God.

He says elsewhere:[44]

> And now we come to the peak of the whole matter . . . The supreme event is Jesus Christ. It is he who is the Word. The Word is no written page. God's words are events; God speaks in events. And therefore the supreme event, the supreme revelation, the supreme word is Jesus Christ . . . The correct way to read the Bible is to begin in the middle with the saving event of Jesus Christ; then go back to the preparation, and then go on to the story of the Church . . .

This sort of statement is also not free from criticism, and certainly Peake (who was more properly an Old Testament scholar) would not have expressed it that way. As a member of the "history of religion" type of interpretation he would have preferred to see the Old Testament standing much more rigidly on its own feet, but nevertheless, he would have rejoiced to see the sheer clarity of Barclay's affirmation of Jesus' centrality thus demonstrated. It is Barclay's most important theological statement, and the key to his theology (not that he had a theological system but, in the sense that he had a working, cohesive body of doctrine of which this was the unitive, linking mechanism). It is the flashpoint, the creative spark between Barclay the Biblical critic, the linguist, the expert on Judaeo-Hellenic custom, culture and literature, and Barclay the devotional writer and commentator.

"I believe in the word of God," he can say,[45] "because in it alone we confront him who is uniquely the Word of God." And even as this christological principle provides the Bible with its unity, so, for Barclay, it gives unity to the faith itself. He can speak,[46] despite his emphasis on the contemporaneity of the faith, of its unchanging quality,

> That is not to say that each age has not to discover the christian faith; but it does say that there is an unchanging nucleus in it — and the permanent centre of it is that Jesus Christ came into the world and lived and died to bring salvation to men.

We said earlier that he was a pragmatic theologian. Here is another proof of that pragmatism which ever explodes into his exposition. He cannot treat of a subject without seeing its immediate applicability. Revelation, Christology, Soteriology: they are all brought into a speedy and inter-connected relationship; Barclay's theology is incapable of standing apart from the world of men: it must be "earthed". Sometimes this happens too quickly; he does not pause to talk through (or to think through?) the meaning and relationships; he declares them, prophetically.

Perhaps we ought to pause to consider the question of where Barclay stands in relation to the views of others, and this cannot be easily done without looking at the often tiresome and misleading question of labels. In a tribute to Barclay at his memorial service in the University of Glasgow, there was a comment on the fact that Barclay was something of an enigma: he was strongly criticised by both liberal and fundamentalist, rejected even by both. This is true. But he was (yet another aspect of his paradoxical position) also acclaimed by them for many things. That also is true. He could berate both liberal and conservative alike; he could agree with both. He cannot truly be numbered with either faction, and it is extremely difficult to place him on the theological map. (The very words liberal and conservative, of course, have no certain definition and are used in widely differing ways.)

David Edwards, in his preface to Barclay's autobiography, prefers to call Barclay's understanding of Christian faith "Liberal Protestantism".[47] But it is not very accurate, either in context of his autobiography or in the light of his many other writings. Says Barclay, "I suppose, if you wish to label me, you would call me a liberal."[48] Many have, and not with the purpose of "placing" him on the theological map, but with the intention of abusing him by it! But does it cover our author? Edwards clearly is aware that it does not do so adequately, and therefore suggests that Barclay's faith might be termed "a layman's faith". I suspect that pleased Barclay — the apostle to the plain man. It should not hide from us that his faith was decisively *evangelical*, and that in a way no self-respecting liberal would wish to be paired with. Not the least aspect of this is the fact that Barclay's faith centred on Jesus, who had come to save men from their sins, and by that act demonstrated the unfailing love of God. Barclay's faith was pragmatic, because the whole Biblical record was pragmatic; it spoke of the dynamic relationship between God and man, and Barclay strove to bear witness to that, and to make it more clearly understood. To do this his attention naturally centred, as the Bible's did, on Jesus himself.

III: A dual activity between God and man

The centre and core is Jesus: the Word of God incarnate. He is the litmus-test of all true doctrine. But how did Barclay handle the question of the Bible's "inspiration"? Had that doctrine any significance for our author beside the central figure of the Biblical record who comes to us today? It is a thorny problem, and bears investigation. It is our third area of his Biblicality; one which he sees as having a dual connotation: the activity of both God and man. Because of this it has interest beyond the simple question of divine inspiration, and impinges on many other aspects. He dealt with it "systematically" in his *Introducing the Bible*,[49] and we follow and précis that account:

1.   His first action was to clear the decks of the misconception, as he saw it, implicit in the question of "verbal inspiration". He does so by simple rejection. He had little sympathy with what Dean Alford called "the suicide theory" of inspiration; that there was any content in the idea of a "dictation" procedure behind the process. (This ability to reject abruptly, without what our industrial psychologists would call "collision cushioning" — that is, conceding before contending — was characteristic, and was one reason for that element of controversy which often surrounded him.) It is unnecessary, both in its psychology and in its reasonableness, for — after all — *any* view of a written account must necessarily be "verbal" in some fashion or other. But reject it he did: it was not a book "fallen down out of heaven". It had a process.

2.   This process he now describes. "The first essential basis of any doctrine of revelation and inspiration is," he affirms, "the Bible, (which) is uniquely the meeting place of the Spirit of God and the spirit of man." He thus presents us early with this crucial aspect of a mutuality of action which is central to his doctrine: the Bible is not to be understood objectively, as it were, in its inspired quality, but in that dynamic relationship of God and man.

3.   That relationship is outlined: the human situation — the setting for the divine activity — is one in which man has used his God-endowed freedom "to turn away from God to himself". (It should be noted here that Barclay is not embarrassed by the term "the Fall", which he uses freely. He does not even try and reinterpret it, as Peake had done before him,

as "a Fall upwards"; it is another part of that innate conservatism of Barclay's).

4.   The next element to be considered is the love of God, which "drives" God to mend the situation. But man's freedom is sovereign; it cannot be impugned. "God cannot intervene directly . . . It is therefore necessary that God should amend the human situation by human instruments." These human instruments were the prophets. "The prophet *is* the man who speaks the word of God; the prophet *is* the inspired man." There is no suggestion as to what the nature of this inspiration might be, still less any elucidation of the mechanics which produced this inspired state. To this we must return.

5.   The characteristics of the prophets are more fully described: they are the conscience of the nation, and are under the absolute control of God, belonging to "his inner council".

6.   A further emphasis on their closeness to the mind of God, insofar as their knowledge of him is obtained first-hand.

7.   That knowledge possesses a moral basis: it is injected with love for God.

8.   Proof of this love is their obedience. The circle has come full turn: the disobedience which wrecked the original design for fellowship between God and man is now turned into willing obedience. "There is a moral element in inspiration," our author declares, without surmising the process which has led from prophetic message to written word.

"We are now coming near to our definition," he continues, "which takes us half-way to our goal":

> An inspired book, a book which is the word of God, is a book which effects a connection between God and man, thereby correcting the human situation, which has gone wrong. It is written by a man who knows God, because he loves God, and whose love has issued in an obedience which fits him to be the instrument of God.

9.   He next makes clear that "for a Jew the revelation of God was not a revelation in words at all; it was a revelation in events". These events, supremely the history of Israel, are the revelation of the divine action, and a large part of the words of the prophets "consists in the interpretation of historical

events". He sees God's hand at work in the event; in the event he sees what God has done, and what God is meaning to say. Therefore —

10. "We can say with complete certainty that the revelation which God gives is given in action and event; and that the Bible is rather the record and the interpretation of these events than revelation in itself. *And now we come to the peak of the whole matter.*

11. "The supreme event, the supreme revelation, the supreme word is Jesus Christ." So we are informed that the Bible is the word of God "because in it and in it alone we are confronted with the life and teaching of Jesus Christ."

It is doubtful if this will do. It has clarified the processes, to some extent at any rate, of God's speaking with man; it has drawn attention to his initiative, and the means he used: the prophets; it has shown that the Bible is *the* record of the events by which the divine will is made known through the interpretations of the prophets; and it has demonstrated the consuming importance of Jesus. But that is statement rather than argument, and we have still not been brought into contact with the real nature of inspiration. The central word in the Pauline vocabulary, for example, *theopneustos*, has not been touched upon (Dr Barclay, so far as I can ascertain, nowhere deals with this unique word), nor does he really come to grips with the two texts (2 Timothy 3:16 and 2 Peter 1:21) which may have thrown light on the problem.

To be sure, he has, once again, highlighted the central importance of Jesus in all this, but he has not really shown *how* these writings differ from any other which also purport to bridge the gap between God and man, and heal the divide created by man's self-assertion. What we have is more an exercise in the criteria of canonicity than an explanation of inspiration. But his assertion is that the Bible *is* inspired, and that it differs from all other books.

Is his understanding of Biblical inspiration one which safeguards the uniqueness of the Bible, its objectivity? It is doubtful, and elsewhere he states that "theologians and the preachers are not the only people who are inspired."[50] He refers to poets, hymnologists, musicians and scientists, all of whom are inspired for all, in different areas and in varying degrees produce "a revelation from God". For "all truth is God's truth". The duality of relationship we saw earlier is repeatedly introduced:

> inspiration depends on two things — the searching mind of man and the revealing Spirit of God . . . In inspiration there is an element that is human and an element which is divine . . .[51]

And in connection with Luke 4:1–4 he shows how this passage spreads particular light on the subject:

> Luke begins by affirming that it is the product of the most careful historical research . . . True inspiration comes when the seeking mind of man joins with the revealing Spirit of God.[52]

Barclay has greatly helped us in seeing something of the human participation involved, but, that apart, the classical understanding and distinctiveness has not really been explored. Like his first aim regarding the miracles, he has sought primarily to explain the happening (*not* explain it away), but one comes away from this account with the sense that something is missing; that the divine involvement has not been handled in the same degree as the human. That for many people is the real problem of inspiration.

IV A contemporary hermeneutic

The final area of his Biblicality concerns his principles of interpretation, his hermeneutical approach. They may thus be summarised:

1. The need for reverence. *Eusebeia* he defines[53] as "reverence in the presence of that which is . . . divine"; or, "The word of true religion"; or "the mark of the Christian

life". It is so in regard to our handling of the scriptures. "So then," he writes,[54] "in the very first place, the reader must bring reverence to the Bible . . . the really Christian study of the scriptures approaches it in an attitude of reverence which is seeking more than grammatical accuracy; it is seeking and finding the grace of God."

2.   We have already seen the supreme place Barclay gave to Jesus. It is no less so as a principle of interpretation; Jesus is its interpretive key: "There is only one way to read the Bible — to read it as all pointing to Jesus Christ . . . the function of the scriptures is not to give life, but to point to him who can."[55]

3.   The activity of the Holy Spirit is recognised as being of paramount importance in the understanding of the Bible, as much as in the writing of it: "The Spirit revealed God's truth to men, and the Spirit enabled men to recognise that truth, when the truth was revealed. So, then, men need the Spirit in their hearts, if they are fully to understand and appropriate the meaning of the word of God."[56] And again, "Scripture is not to be interpreted by private cleverness or private prejudice; it is to be interpreted by the help of the Holy Spirit, by whom it was first given."[57]

4.   Barclay has a high concept of the Church, which impinges upon this area, too. "To study Scripture wisely we must study it within the tradition of the Church," he maintains. "It would be a matter of folly — and arrogant folly at that — if when we came to the study of any passage of Scripture we completely neglected all that the scholarship and the devotion of the past had learned about it." And elsewhere he can tartly say: "There is either an almost incredible arrogance or an almost unbelievable naïveté in the person who feels no need of any help in the interpretation of Scripture. . . . No sane and reverent person can ever think of studying Scripture, as it were, outside the Church." He is aware of the dangers that this view could support, but is insistent that it is the correct one and those dangers will be offset by taking into account "the whole view of Scripture".

5.   We have seen that his view of the compilation of the Bible was a dynamic one: "If the Bible story stretches over scores of centuries, there cannot be in it one flat level of thought and religion and ethics. There is bound to be development."[58] He

owns that some aspects of the Bible are "sub-Christian".[59] The Bible must be understood in the light of this process, this evolution, on the principle of the earlier giving way to the later, the lower to the higher.

6.   The Bible is a literary work, and must be treated as such. Its vehicle is language, therefore "the beginning of our study must be the study of words".[60] This is what Harnack called "scavenger's labour" and Barclay was a past-master of its techniques and discipline. "Words are fascinating things," he said,[61] and showed by an unfailing devotion to them just what he meant. His books scintillate with word-studies; he is not afraid to give the original, whether it be Hebrew, Greek, Aramaic, Latin or whatever: but it is not lauded or inflicted on his readers, but quietly slipped in, explained, and used as an intelligent lever into the original writer's mind. It is in this area most of all that we would dissent from his self-criticism of having "a second-class mind". He was ever particularly at home with languages, and some of his expositions were highly creative because of this. Luther was wont to say that "theology is grammar"; this true son of the Reformation took the logic one step further back, and showed that initially it was in *words*.

7.   There are great dangers in the isolation of single words and passages, of which he was well aware. We have seen that his defence against an over-assertive Church tradition is to assert "the whole view of Scripture". He was ever ready to underline the importance of reading whole tracts and passages: "It would be well if we could stop treating the Bible as a book of lessons and problems, and read it simply as a book with the most moving and thrilling story on earth to tell."[62] For the same reason he was critical of the comparatively recent innovation of verse and chapter divisions, and suggested modern versions which avoided this pitfall.

So we have it: a man inspired and motivated by the study of this one Book, in whose hands the text never failed to come alive; through his reverence for it, his humbly seeking after the truth of its divine author, aided by all the benefits of linguistic, historical and literary research. He produced from it a stream of commentaries and monographs which even the young or those in different cultures from our own could understand and enjoy, and who never failed to be fresh and relevant. Let his be the last word on this unique Book:

> There is no book which cost so much as the Bible. Today it is in serious danger of deserving the cynical definition of a classic — a book of which everyone has heard and which no one has read. We have the privilege of possessing the Bible and that privilege is a responsibility for which we shall answer.

Notes

1. A comprehensive list of these will be found in my *Men and Affairs* (Mowbrays, 1978). There is one significant omission: Barclay's first book, which seems to have escaped everyone's attention till now (except in the Church of Scotland *Fasti*), including the author who referred to *Ambassador for Christ* as his first volume. That is not so. *New Testament Studies* was published in 1937 by the Scottish Sunday School Union for Christian Education and was Barclay's 'literary firstborn'. Despite its title, which is rather pretentious as it is a fairly simple guide to some key aspects of mainly the Gospel writings, there is no academic interest or framework, and the style — clearly recognisable as William Barclay's — is very conservative theologically. His real book career certainly commenced with *Ambassador for Christ*, in 1951, just four years after he took up his university lectureship at Glasgow.
2. *Seen in the passing*, p. 15. Edited by Rita F. Snowden (Collins, 1966; it has more recently been reissued under the title *In the hands of God*, 1977). My italics.
3. *Testament of Faith*, p. 35. (Mowbrays, 1975).
4. The phrase used by the *Methodist Recorder* reviewing the revised edition of the DSB on September 18, 1975. Whilst the series cannot be described as a technical work, it clearly is the author's major work.
5. DSB: *The Gospel of Matthew*, vol. I, p.v. The point is made in each of the seventeen volumes.
6. *Recollections and Appreciations*, p. 28. Edited by W. F. Howard (Epworth Press, 1938).
7. *Men and Affairs* p. 59.

8. *A Commentary on the Bible*, p. xii (Nelsons, 1919). The volume was completely revised, under the editorship of H. H. Rowley and M. Black and reissued in 1963; it was retitled *Peake's Commentary on the Bible.*
9. *Recollections and Appreciations*, p. 85. The quote which follows is from p. 161.
10. Inaugural Lectures delivered by Members of the Faculty of Theology, p. vii. Edited by A. S. Peake (Manchester University, 1905).
11. Ad loc.
12. *Bulletin of the John Rylands Library*, vol. xiv. I, (January 1930).
13. Testament of Faith, p. 101.
14. *On Literature*, p. 130 (New English Library, 1967).
15. Note 1, above.
16. Testament of Faith, p. 93.
17. Op. cit., p. 24.
18. *Testament of Faith*, p. 58.
19. DSB: *The Gospel of Matthew*, vol. I, p. 338.
20. Op. cit., p. 361.
21. Op. cit., p. 323.
22. DSB: *The Gospel of John*, vol. I, p. 192.
23. DSB: *The Letters to Timothy, Titus and Philemon*, p. 200.
24. DSB: *The Gospel of Mark*, p. 123. A comparison of *New Testament Studies* and *Testament of Faith* shows some of the development in his thinking.
25. Op. cit. p. 317.
26. *Testament of Faith*, p. 6.
27. "I am a simple-minded person. I have neither a philosophical nor a theological mind." Op. cit., p. 34.
28. *And Jesus Said*, p. 11.
29. Cf. "With the name of Pilate the events of Jesus' death are firmly anchored in history." *The Plain Man Looks at the Apostles' Creed*, p. 90. (Collins, 1967). The present quote is from his autobiography, p. 108.
30. Testament of Faith, p. 48.
31. *Biblical Studies: Essays in Honour of William Barclay*, p. 9. Edited by Johnston R. McKay and James F. Miller (Collins, 1976).
32. Op. cit., "Barclay the Broadcaster", p. 25.
33. p. 89. (The book was published jointly by The Bible Reading Fellowship and the International Bible Reading Association in 1972; it is available from the National Christian Education Council.)

34. Op. cit., p. 11.
35. *The Making of the Bible*, p. 10. (Lutterworth Press, 1961; recently reissued by The Saint Andrew Press.)
36. DSB: *The Letter to the Hebrews*, p. 200.
37. *Introducing the Bible*, p. 93.
38. DSB: *The Letter to the Hebrews*, p. 39.
39. *Testament of Faith*, p. 90.
40. *And He had Compassion*, p. 3. (The Saint Andrew Press, 1975).
41. DSB: *The Letters to Timothy, Titus and Philemon*, p. 201.
42. DSB: *The Letters of James and Peter*, p. 337.
43. *Testament of Faith*, pp. 48f.
44. *Introducing the Bible*, 146f.
45. Op. cit., p. 147.
46. DSB: *The Letters of John and Jude*, p. 178.
47. *Testament of Faith*, p. xi.
48. *Seen in the Passing*, p. 153.
49. pp. 137–148; a chapter which bears the positive title, "The Inspired Book".
50. DSB: *The Gospel of John*, vol. II, p. 195.
51. DSB: *The Letters of James and Peter*, p. 180.
52. DSB: *The Gospel of Luke*, p. 8.
53. *New Testament Words*, pp. 111f.
54. *Introducing the Bible*, p. 90.
55. DSB: *The Gospel of John*, vol. I, p. 198.
56. *Introducing the Bible*, pp. 107f.
57. DSB: *The Letters of James and Peter*, p. 313.
58. *Introducing the Bible*, p. 112.
59. ibid.
60. Op. cit., p. 101.
61. *New Testament Words*, p. 11.
62. *Communicating the Gospel*, p. 52.

7 – Portrait of a scholar and colleague
by Neil Alexander

Neil Alexander is now minister of St. Andrew's in Rome, the Scots church serving an international Reformed protestant congregation. But from 1964 to 1978 he worked closely with William Barclay in the same department of the Divinity Faculty at Glasgow University, as lecturer and later senior lecturer in New Testament Language and Literature. Brought up in a manse on the main road between Glasgow and Barclay's home town of Motherwell, Neil Alexander was a parish minister in this Lanarkshire steel country, at Cambuslang on the fringe of Glasgow, before becoming a lecturer in Biblical Criticism at Aberdeen University. As a Glasgow student, before going on to the Union Theological Seminary at New York, he sat under Barclay, but later came to know him as scholar and university colleague as well as professor and friend.

I – Barclay as Scholar: much more than "impeccable linguistics"

The general public had no doubts: William Barclay was a great scholar. In the face of his many books and countless lectures a vast lay readership and audience was spell-bound by his fluency, and personality, by the mass of factual information and the range of reference and illustration he lavishly and effortlessly poured out. How could anyone doubt that such a man was a scholar — and a great one?

William Barclay himself was none too sure of it. Ainslie McIntyre and I, for many years his lecturers, may not have taken him too seriously when he used to say: "Of course, I know I'm not the scholar you are — either of you — but . . ."

(and then add, with discomfiting implications, that he had no doubt about being able to *teach!*). Doubt of his scholarship dogged him throughout his career. Never did he speak in my hearing of his lack of a Ph.D. — which, from just before the time he had been brought upon the academic scene, was becoming almost obligatory as a passport to university teaching — but there were signs that it irked. A richly deserved honorary doctorate of divinity eventually came along but that was something different.

Reaction to this lack of any earned higher degree (especially, I think, of one gained outside Scotland) best accounts for some curious judgments of his over the years. He overvalued the attainment and experience he did *not* have and the type of man they might have made him, and was too impressed by them in others. Again and again he would show quite misplaced admiration for some smooth, slick, career-academic's "culture" (whatever he meant by that), or another's thesis-like tome, overloaded with footnotes and obscurity. When, quite late in his career, he had entrée to Oxford, it was enough to make him quite silly about there being "no comparison between the scholarship of Oxbridge and that of our Scottish universities": he felt "quite uneducated down there". And one of his unrealised notions, shortly before he retired, was of submitting (as he must have been assured he might do) a collection of his more "academic" writings to Oxford for consideration for a doctorate. Success in this would at last, as it were, prove him a real scholar to himself. And, as he even then felt need, to the scholastic world.

William Barclay's colleagues in Scotland never showed themselves unambiguously convinced that he was a scholar. At a crucial time for him, in fact, he must have been driven to conclude that, strictly as an "academic", he did not have their confidence.

By 1963 he had been first Lecturer, then Senior Lecturer, in New Testament Language and Literature in Glasgow University in the Department of Divinity and Biblical Criticism for a total of seventeen years, with resounding success. When Professor G. H. C. Macgregor retired, William Barclay — to his students past and present and to his vast public following — was the obvious, surely inevitable, man to succeed to the vacant Chair. Right enough, he was appointed.

The process, however, had been agonisingly slow and incredibly painful. I was never again to see William Barclay so distraught as when I met him during this protracted ordeal. He felt "every man's hand was against him", as reports leaked of opposition to him in the appointing committee. His theological views were deemed suspect (or worse) by some. It more deeply wounded him that his academic fitness for the job was also questioned. As we have seen, he knew that "on paper" he was vulnerable here. What rankled, I am sure, was the discounting of his universally-acclaimed seventeen-year teaching record in the department as the Professor's right hand man: that — and, no doubt, the belittling of his books. The cry of such an appointing committee is: "Published Works!" Alas, what it means by that and what William Barclay had did not coincide. (To be fair to the committee, he must have been thoroughly well aware that this would be so.) The committee would be looking, from any would-be Professor, for publications of highly technical, specialised material, esteemed (and often only estimable) by fellow-experts. (Suitable slighter offerings might be *Malchus's Ear: The Case for the Left* or *The Minoan Background of the New Testament* or *The Beast: Was He a She?*) Already by 1963 William Barclay had had prodigious output (and sales) in the New Testament field; these very books, in the absence of those others, of an arcane, esoteric type, hindered rather than helped his candidacy. They were "popular". So, the evidence strongly suggested that his academic limits were those of his books.

At long last, William Barclay's cause won through, thanks (hearsay has it) to his *Educational Ideas in the Ancient World* — his one volume reckoned "academically respectable" in its "weight" — and to a finally over-riding awareness in the committee that *not* to appoint this remarkable man, this genius of a teacher, this long-proven unstintingly-dedicated servant of both his Church and his university, would be scandalous. Theoretically, appointment to this illustrious Chair should have dispelled all his doubt about standing as a scholar. In practice, his appointment, coming so begrudged by his clerical and academic peers, was to keep this alive to the end of his days.

It kept him, scholastically speaking, humble for the remaining ten years of his university career. The humility worked in him in two ways. On the one hand, he had never sought, nor did he then begin to seek, to impose his scholarly views on others. Always, he would agree to disagree. Apart from his love of peace, I think there was here genuine acceptance that this other chap, odd as his notions were, might be a better "scholar". On the other hand, his humility gave him a sense of awed responsibility. As a Scot in the New Testament field at this level, there were various mantles from the past waiting for him to assume — such as those of his immediate predecessor G. H. C. Macgregor, and of James Denney and James Moffatt: mighty Scottish contributors, of international repute, to New Testament study. Could he wear them? (It would have been quite uncharacteristic of him to speak in such terms, nor did he ever so speak to me but he gave the impression he felt this question, which *any* appointee would feel in this professorship, with a special keenness.)

I think he admitted to himself, right from the time of his appointment in 1963, that, strictly speaking, he never *could* wear these mantles. At the same time, he correctly judged that he already had a mantle of his own, right for the kind of man and the kind of scholar he *would* claim to be. And he set himself to make it, in its own way, more and more fit to join these others which were, so to speak, lying beside his desk, profoundly influencing him, all the time driving him on, through the next ten years.

The last three sentences come as close as I can bring the reader to indicating William Barclay's humble sense of "awed responsibility" in that professorial office. They also lead us, in as helpful a way as I can find, towards the truth about William Barclay as scholar.

Yes, he *was* a scholar, but, as every aspect of him requires us to say, one *sui generis*: an absolutely unique "mix". We shall try to see the scholar by looking at the whole "mix". But it should be said at the outset that two deficiencies bar him, overall, from highest rating as a scholar. He lacked any *philosophic bent* and he lacked the *power* (or perhaps only failed to take the opportunity) *to grow*.

Much Biblical criticism has been put in bondage to modern philosophy; he dutifully read it but it was an alien, unfriendly world for him. He got nothing useful out of it for himself nor anything he felt the urge, or competence, to communicate or condemn. Again, he leaves no evidence of having grown over his long years of academic life. His own theology and Biblical criticism of 1946 (which, like most parish ministers, were those of his student days — i.e. in his case liberal and Source-critical) never significantly altered to assimilate the measure of truth within such trends as Neo-orthodoxy, Biblical Theology, Form-Criticism and Redaction Criticism. He read them up, he passed them on faithfully enough, but none really caught fire in his own mind. They never entered into the essential William Barclay. In 1974 he was still a liberal, however much he latterly protested he was now a fundamentalist! We might explain this apparent stagnation by his forever writing and speaking — yes, and reading; his never stopping, simply to reflect and change and grow. (I am sure that was what Professor Macgregor meant when he remarked to me, in 1959, "He's a first-rate colleague . . . an amazing man . . . great chap . . . I just wish he'd stop writing books for a while.") Whatever the cause, it was a deficiency which would, I think, keep him from a placing in the top flight of scholars.

But the "strangeness" of William Barclay, putative scholar, lay above all in his turn of mind and style of speech (and, often, writing). These were not those of any orthodox "scholarly man". For example, he seemed indifferent to, even incapable of, the cautious, word-weighing, pro-and-conning, *modus cogitandi, parlandi* and *scribendi* of the classic scholar. Typically with him, things were "completely, absolutely and utterly" this or that! And before a popular audience (e.g. on television) or in a press interview, when "scholars" would feel responsibility to be more than ordinarily judicious, he seemed to go out of his way to show himself master of the incautious hyperbolic expression. (Exact enough to be a sample, I believe, are these remembered, hair-raisingly perilous, final words in a Barclay television programme: "Jesus came to show us that sins don't matter.") Desire to rivet attention, to startle, even shock? That was a factor. But it was, above all, how his mental processes worked.

The typical "scholar" is unable to think of only one factor, one side of an issue at one time. His training and temperament insist on his seeing a problem in balance, even if it is a balance of tension. Not so William Barclay! His was a passionate absorption, at any moment, in a single facet of truth then facing him in speaking or writing; to be communicated, as he then saw it, and felt it, without any qualification or *caveat* whatsoever. Next week on the screen or two pages later in his book he would present with equally single-minded passion (again as if the whole truth) some other facet, often bearing every appearance of being diametrically opposed to the first! And he seemed oblivious of need to accommodate them somehow to each other.

Such an extraordinary "one-off" kind of mind! Yet, there seems at least one equivalent sensibility after all! Peter Dobereiner in the *Observer*, (May 13, 1979) wrote on Gary Player:

> When you get to know him you realise that he brings the same passionate conviction to every opinion he expresses, down to giving his preference for French mustard over the English variety on his steak. And the next week, dare I mention, he may well produce a spell-binding condemnation of French mustard on the grounds that it rots the liver while extolling English mustard as no less than the elixir of life.
>
> But on the first meeting it would take a quite exceptional cynic to doubt one syllable of his utterance.

Those who knew William Barclay best will say: "Pure Willie!" That Gary Player thinks and speaks like that does not affect his golf or his status as a professional golfer. The same attribute in William Barclay could not be irrelevant to his professionalism as scholar.

But look now at what else went into the "mix" of Professor William Barclay! He graduated Master of Arts with First Class Honours in classics at Glasgow University and went on to gain a Bachelor of Divinity degree with Distinction in New Testament in the Faculty of Divinity. (Distinction was, in those days, the highest award that could be given in Divinity, there being then no B.D. Honours degree.)

With these degrees (the B.D., of course, including Hebrew), William Barclay possessed the indispensably right tools of the finest calibre for what proved to be his job for most of his working life, as a New Testament scholar and teacher.

There is much more in that sentence than perhaps meets the eye. First: "the indispensably right tools" for professing New Testament are the classics: classical Latin and classical (Attic) Greek. A working knowledge of New Testament (*koinē*) Greek alone, picked up in the course of theological studies, is just not good enough to make a man authoritative or reliable as a scholar in the field. "He knows not Greek who only *koinē* knows." The ancient Greek ancestry of the New Testament language (along with the Hebrew-influenced usages of Greek in the Septuagint and usages in secular Hellenistic Greek) again and again sheds needed light, and always has to be allowed for, whenever translation and exposition are made. Further: no matter how New Testament studies may develop, nothing — neither English, nor Philosophy, nor French, nor German nor anything else — can ever displace the classics as the essential basic equipment of any *Neutestamenter*.

William Barclay had this equipment — the indispensable tools. And they were of the finest calibre. Honours in classics in Glasgow was overwhelmingly a linguistic degree. It meant, in those days, mastery of the Latin and Greek Languages in minutest detail and command of huge tracts of Latin and Greek texts, representative of the great variety in form, style, date, etc., of their literatures. For his required special subject in his Honours, I believe, William Barclay opted for Hellenistic Greek (i.e. the Greek, both secular and Biblical, of the New Testament era). This extended still further the linguistic demand and range of his Greek "profession".* This was the classical linguistic marathon in which William Barclay got a First. Long years lay ahead in which the fruits of his highest distinction in this most rigorous and exacting linguistic

*For some time after appointment in 1946 to his Lectureship in New Testament in Trinity College, William Barclay was also Lecturer in Hellenistic Greek in the University's Faculty of Arts.

discipline were to be poured out, without stint, in all his books and lectures, for his students' — and, it virtually seemed, a whole world's — enlightening. William Barclay was a New Testament scholar all right. In this vital area of New Testament *language* — of establishing precisely what the words mean and how we should interpret them in order to be faithful to what their writer intended — his contribution has been tremendous and always has carried the weight of his undoubted linguistic authority. "The indispensably right tools . . . of the finest calibre" William Barclay possessed and wielded supremely well in this part of his academic job as New Testment scholar and teacher. Can there be any part more important?

He "possessed" these tools, I wrote earlier. The verb was chosen through failure to find a better. It is not good enough but it must serve. "Had" would be totally inadequate. Our ears know, to their displeasure, and in the case of some of us to our shame, that not every one who "has" an L.R.A.M. is a musician. And there is a kind of doctrinal indoctrination which can produce a thoroughly informed orthodox "believing" that makes no difference to the "believer" in himself. He could have, as it were, a degree in the faith — he "has" the faith — but he is no Christian! The nature of classics, "dead" languages — and the stringently linguistic, stylistic and grammatical, form of the Glasgow Honours classics requirement at that time made it particularly possible that a student of exceptional industry, perseverance, motivation and memory could master the techniques and meet the requirement — even to the point of gaining a First — with minimal absorption of anything beyond the linguistics themselves.

I have known just such classics Firsts from my own time; they "had" classics, but despite the substance of the texts they read, and the Greek and Roman turns of mind revealed in the linguistics, and the styles of life pointed to in their literatures, they had neither found fascination nor ever really assimilated them. Such fascination and assimilation are precisely the mark of that rare bird, the real classical scholar, who *cannot* forget his classics after the finals! He "possesses" them, not merely "has" them, in that these "dead" languages have come alive in himself and become part of himself and these ancient "dead" peoples have become for him as real and known as the folks next door. Just such a first-rate, authentic classical scholar was William Barclay.

Through the door to which the languages alone gave the key, he entered into, and freely moved about in, the whole Graeco-Roman world. It was as much his home as Merrylea, as much his parish as Renfrew, as much his *patris* as Wick or even Motherwell! I can think of no-one else in our generation who has had just such a feeling for, as well as commanding erudition about, the culture of that Graeco-Roman world, which (with a special place within it for Judaism) is, of course, the background-world of the New Testament.

As a student in Arts, he had been required for his degree to read widely in that background world — but he would need no goad to read. He was a voracious reader all his life and a phenomenally fast one. And, until his final years, he was blessed with a memory still more phenomenal, for everything once read. In his university teaching, he could pull just the right references out of the air, as it were — from Cicero or Quintilian or Demosthenes or Thucydides (or the papyri), never looked at since his student days; or from the Church Fathers, whose mostly tedious, voluminous works he somewhat later also made it his business to "possess"; or from Philo, Josephus or the Talmud!

With prodigality he was to illuminate his lectures and his writings for the general public (not least the *Daily Study Bible*) with this or that fresh, though ancient, illustration, to point a telling contrast with the early Christian *ethos* or to explain, by its reference to some first-century Greek or Roman (or Jewish) custom, or legal or religious practice — to explain with an effectiveness nothing else could have had — precisely the point of an enigmatic New Testament verse.

So it is not sufficient to say of William Barclay that his scholarly contribution was limited to his impeccable linguistics. He was also a great "Introduction and Background" New Testament scholar. His exploitation (in the term's best sense) and application of his knowledge of classical (especially Latin, perhaps) literature and culture in the interests of New Testament study have been immense. His sheer *revelling* in this particular area of scholarly work gets across to even the reader of his printed pages, as it certainly did to his viewers and his students. It would be wrong to *under-rate*, on that account, the solid actual substance of his achievement in this area. Coolly and objectively appraised, it is indeed immense; always reliable, always useful and helpful, often unforgettably clarifying.

There, then, is the extraordinary "mix" of Professor William Barclay. William Barclay the scholar is an essential part of the "mix". He was a scholar of the highest quality, in two of the most fundamental aspects of New Testament scholarship.

II – Barclay as Colleague: vitality, diversity, and a passionate love of teaching

"Just call me Willie. Everyone else does!" (True, though Mrs Barclay always called him Bill.) Thus I was greeted on my first day as lecturer to the newly-appointed Professor Barclay in 1964.

I had been a student of his when he was inducted to his Lectureship in 1946 and had benefited greatly from his enthusiastic, lavishly informative and lucid teaching and from his encouragement of my own student work throughout the remainder of my course. He had taken a kindly interest in my going to New York in 1948 to study and in my settlement in 1949 in a parish in Cambuslang. But, from 1948 to 1964, especially after I went to Aberdeen University to teach in 1955, our contracts were very few and far between, though always enjoyed. In that period, of course, William Barclay had become one of the best-known names in Scotland; inevitably I came to know a lot *about* him over these years. But probably I knew *him* in 1964 only a little more closely than in my student days. That had been more close than I had come to know any other who had taught me in Divinity, simply because Mr Barclay had — towards all the students — a forthcomingness and positive friendliness that marked a new departure in staff-student relations.

Clearly, when I returned to be a colleague, my Professor Barclay was still the Mr Barclay who had taught me — even if he had put on both weight and colour. "Just call me Willie." That set the tone for the next ten years.

We were to disagree on virtually every doctrine at some time or other in the years ahead. I did not let him away with his irresponsible heresy or schoolmasterish legalism! He thought my theology sadly orthodox and my ethics dangerously radical ("pure anarchy!"). And we were to disagree from time to time over the wisdom of bright ideas he would come up with for changing teaching policy or over, in my opinion, the laxness with which he was handling some "weak brother" of a student. But I have never met a man whose goodwill and geniality remained so completely unimpaired by impassioned argument and repeated contradiction of his views. He was "Willie" — and Willie was incapable of rancour.

Two sets of people have asked me regularly down the years: "What's it like working closely with, and under, William Barclay?" The first are members of the general public. Their question has been put with awe and envy in the voice. It was impossible to fail to feel that they thought of our relationship (i.e. of Ainslie McIntyre, latterly also John Riches, and myself) to Willie being most closely paralleled by that of Peter, James and John to Jesus! (Such was the reverence the public has had for Willie that this parallel is robbed of irreverence.) They were completely wrong if this meant, as I suspect it often did, that we were uniquely privileged by our closeness to Willie's "holy glow". Willie's *charisma* was powerful but it was no "holy glow" and he would have shuddered at any thought that he might have one! (The only times I've known him sound false have been final moments on television programmes when he felt called to "wind up" with some pietistic *mot*.)

In fact, at close quarters he was "of the earth, earthy", even too earthy occasionally, but utterly, delightfully human withal.

What impressed most the "inner disciples" was his passionate love of his teaching work, the unbelievable vitality and shaming industry of the man (three books on the go at the same time, at least once), the diversity of interesting associations he had and people he met and "raconted" about, the preposterously provocative statements (*"The Scottish Daily Express?* I believe every word"*) on anything under the sun which enlivened every conversation, and the bonhomie pervading it all. This first set of people with their question were way off the beam about any "holy glow" but they were absolutely right in their assumption that Ainslie McIntyre, John Riches and I were highly privileged people. We were, and we knew it.

The other set of people who have frequently asked me this question were Glasgow University teachers, particularly my own Divinity colleagues in other departments. They have tended to put the question commiseratingly, as if they believed it must be a great trial to work under this unconventional, unpredictable man, with a thousand extra-mural irons in the fire and about as many ideas (some of them eccentric if not heretical, some of them "here today and gone tomorrow" even in his own thinking) buzzing in his head and ready on the tongue — on New Testament matters and everything else.

These people were far further off the mark than the first set of questioners. Possibly they misjudged *me*, in the first place! I am not really so sober and conventional as to have been put off by Willie's impulsive deviations from the norm or so sold on logic and consistency as to have been *deeply* upset by his "Playerism". Much more surely, they underestimated the love which Willie evoked. It indubitably covered a multitude of sins — even the wildest of notions and the least tasteful of "humorous" anecdotes.

Above all, they completely underrated his powers as manager of departmental affairs: the actual distribution and discharge of teaching and examining duties and of administrative and pastoral obligations towards individual students: and his management of *us*, his junior and subordinate colleages.

Various points stand out in memory which illustrate my claim that he was an excellent head of the department and the easiest of "bosses".

Never did I know him to miss a lecture in order to take up some outside engagement, however prestigious or lucrative. Never was he behind in the chores of drawing up and marking exam papers and in arrangements with external examiners.

However busy he was — on the next book, on his *British Weekly* or *Expository Times* or *Life and Work* page, on his script for radio (his television was unscripted), on this or that article or review — he was never "too busy"; without fail he was accessible, graciously and welcomingly so, to his colleagues, or students, or anyone else who called. (A scholar with a comparable work-output who had been the same was Professor Archie Hunter in Aberdeen.) We who served under him always knew, in good time, on just what we were to lecture and where and when we were to do it. However erratic in other ways Willie may have been, in all these ways he was perfectly consistent and business-like. He made his arrangements with us and kept to them; he trusted us and left us to carry out *our* part. As a result, we had justly the repute among the students of being a department second to none in the faculty for being "well-run".

He was a model to his two, latterly three, colleagues in his sheer love of lecturing to students. He expended his energies on that without stint, right to the end going carefully over his prepared material beforehand. (The response to his lectures, especially in the large first-year classes in which students were being given their first taste of critical New Testament study at university level, was tremendous. He communicated his own passion for his subject and he captivated them.) He shared none of the doubt of some academics that his basic task as a university teacher was to *teach*! To me, too, that is beyond dispute. And *how* he taught not only inspired his hearers but set a standard for his colleagues which rebuked, as well as inspired, *us*.

He managed his New Testament colleagues, as distinct from the departmental work, with no less success, in my judgment. Willie had the advantage of coming into university teaching with many years of dealing with people in his effective pastorate in Renfrew, and in the university (unlike some who in the old days were shot straight out of the pulpit into a Chair) he had gone the whole way, step by step, from Lecturer (Church), Lecturer (University), to Senior Lecturer and Professor. He understood from first hand a Lecturer's anxieties and aspirations. When he became Professor he did not forget. This unforgotten experience together with his freedom from any sense of scholastic superiority over his colleagues, kept him from the kind of hurtful *gaffe* which other Divinity Professors — without this experience and without this modesty — have been known to commit: that of making an out-dated sharp divide between Professors and those they referred to as "junior members of faculty". Willie could never have done that! Yet he was the Professor — and we knew it. He told us what we were all going to do and we did it. The atmosphere was one in which we could easily have demurred at something unreasonable being demanded of us and, like a shot, Willie would have adjusted matters, but I have no memory of the occasion ever arising. Perhaps Willie was anachronistic in his methods here — which were much more those of benevolent paternalism (never despotism!) than of joint consultation (*de rigeur* today), but I confess I found them ideal, just as similar treatment by Professor G. H. C. Macgregor had made Willie feel he had the perfect boss.

It was a "benevolent" paternalism, in the extreme. The hospitality of Willie to his departmental staff is legendary. Any departmental business was done not in his room or in office hours but after dinner at the Overseas League Club (now defunct in Glasgow), the College Club or the Royal Scottish Automobile Club. Latterly that was the favourite place. Well wined and dined — our envious colleagues in other departments said — we would agree to anything! There (against the club rules, I believe) our business was transacted. The division of labour would be mapped out for a whole term, even whole year, ahead. There, too, one of the heftiest academic-administrative jobs there was, heftier every year as course options in Divinity multiplied, that of making up a host of degree exam papers for June and September, was tackled. Before the night was out it was well on the road to being finished; sometimes we actually left with the work complete. The tedium of what we had had to do was remarkably lightened by the comfort and the cuisine of our meeting-place. The fact that we agreed so easily on the business before us and got ahead with it so well may owe something to our relaxing preconditioning!

The external examiner was similarly "softened", as cynical observers used to put it, but, in all fairness to Willie, the examiner was, like ourselves, the lucky victim not of the host's guile but of his generosity.

By this time it should be thoroughly evident that departmental affairs, in and out of university premises, were conducted in an entirely congenial social atmosphere in which (however vigorous our wordy warfare over theological matters), on a personal level "never was heard a discouraging word". Thanks to Willie, it was a joy to be home on that range!

Only once, so far as I know, did I do or say anything that hurt Willie's feelings. It was unwittingly done, of course, but that made the hurt no less — or less regretted. It was not caused by my exposure of some glaring logical fallacy in a position he was espousing. To that sort of wound, regularly inflicted, he was impervious! It happened in 1965 in the College Club (the University staff club) where I found him at a coffee-table with Sir Charles Illingworth, Regius Professor of Surgery at that time, one of the closest of Willie's many university friends outside the Divinity Faculty. Willie asked me to join them. I was introduced to Illingworth, who asked, "What's Willie like as a boss? Quite a handful, I'd think." It was jokingly asked and invited a jocular reply.

So, in the same light, bantering vein, I said Willie was "a terrible taskmaster . . . a real slave-driver . . .": the kind of thing which one can say without offence among friends and only because it is something too preposterous to be taken seriously. So I thought. But, as soon as we were alone, Willie was on to it: urgent, anxious and upset. "Is that really so? Am I honestly like that?" I rushed to reassure him but it took a lot of doing. I was, as they say, mortified. Over the years I learned to understand why Willie had so strongly reacted. I found that, rarely as he judged, his severest judgment, by far, of some scholar as a person, was: "He is not a *kind* man." That he himself might be thought to have fallen under the same condemnation had horrified him. For him — and was it not so for the Man he followed? — unkindness was the real sin against the Holy Ghost.

Negatively, Willie's conviction of this found expression in the truth about him that my wife (Willie's secretary from 1969–1974) voiced on the day of his death: "He had not a malicious bone in his body."

Positively, as a man and, more specifically, as a colleague, his priorities were exactly right. With that very consistency and perfectionism he lamentably scorned in scholarship, he adamantly adhered to these priorities. William Barclay ("Just call me Willie") was — *always* was — the very personification of kindness of heart and generosity of mind and spirit.

8 – Barclay as broadcaster
by Ronald Falconer
with a postscript by Douglas Aitken

Any study of William Barclay as a communicator and a personality has to take account of his success as a broadcaster and especially his dramatic impact, late in life, on television. He appeared to break many of the rules, or belie many of the assumptions, of TV communication. He reached a wide audience which rarely went to church.

But the spoken word and the TV image are inevitably ephemeral. Not all of those who manage their production have the insight or sensitivity to understand what they have achieved or failed to achieve, or why. Dr. Ronald Falconer, brought up in New Zealand but educated back in Scotland at Aberdeen University and ordained in the Church of Scotland, was for twenty-six years head of religious broadcasting in Scotland for the British Broadcasting Corporation. He was an outstanding producer (and radiant Christian) who did understand and who saw religious broadcasting as part of the evangelism of the Christian community, the Church. He died a few months before Barclay but his account of their partnership in television is bound to be the definitive account of how an ageing professor, who had once been warned that his Clydeside accent would prevent him from "getting on in the Church", made a brilliant success of TV lectures delivered without trimmings or gimmicks. Falconer's account first appeared in his posthumously published autobiography, The Kilt beneath my Cassock *(The Handsel Press, Edinburgh). It follows here with a few amendments, mainly deletions of references to local Scottish places or programmes or internal BBC matters. For Falconer, Barclay was supremely "the man for the common man".*

Every so often in broadcasting, someone comes along who breaks all the rules. In radio, the voice is all-important. It should be attractive to listen to, well modulated with clear enunciation but in a natural way. Such voices were common BBC practice until the rather ugly — to me — English regional accents began to dominate. Friendly voices too, like Ronald Selby Wright's during the War years, or Tom Allan's, or David Easton's or quite a few of those who gave such splendid contributions to the Radio Missions of 1950 and 1952. Yet that roll of radio honour does not contain the name of perhaps the greatest communicator of them all, William Barclay.

We "discovered" him shortly afterwards. He was already well known as a writer on New Testament themes and had become a Lecturer in Trinity College, Glasgow. But as a broadcaster, he broke all the rules. He had a harsh-sounding voice; his speech poured out in an endless stream with few pauses; his Scots accent was thick and guttural. Yet there was a dynamic quality about him which made people listen. And what he was saying was informative, lit with countless illustrations drawn straight from life, and above all, expressed in terms which the ordinary man could understand. He made the New Testament *live*. I remember producing one of his early "People's Services" from a church on the outskirts of Glasgow. Jerry Girot, my Outside Broadcast engineer, was a lively R.C. whose repartee was a byword in BBC-Scotland. Willie Barclay was holding forth on the five Greek words which reveal the various degrees of *Sin* in the New Testament, beginning with his complaint that English was a poverty-stricken language. It had only one word for sin, while the Greeks had five. Jerry was much impressed: in his own words, Willie hadn't missed him and hit the wall!

Willie was best in the popular spaces, "The People's Service" on the Light Programme, "Lift Up Your Hearts" on Home Service. One "Lift Up" talk so gripped a young woman on the verge of committing suicide that she sought him out and was able to take a saner look at life as a result. It was all very remarkable, for certainly Willie Barclay would never have passed a BBC Audition test.

I was sure he could become a television personality as on

radio, but Willie would have none of it. Twice yearly I wrote him, offering him a broadcast; twice yearly he replied saying "No". He confessed frankly that he was afraid of the cameras and did not see his rugged self cut out for this sort of thing. Then one day he wrote to say his wife Kate was calling him a coward and that he would have a go. But please could he have some of his beloved students with him in the studio to make him feel at home. So we devised a format in which he expounded some commonplace aspects of the New Testament, then answered their questions. The students were a well-chosen group, some being older men who had entered the Ministry late in life, others more normal, including one who was brilliant academically and articulate into the bargain.

The series was recorded in 1962. The moment we saw Willie through the camera, all of us, production staff, engineers cameramen, knew we had a winner in television terms. My colleagues were fascinated by this ebullient character out of whom spilled knowledge, humour, real-life stories, common sense, and all with an intensely human appeal. The viewers thought the same and wrote in to say so. It was the day of the argumentative, over-intellectualised "Meeting Point" programmes. He doesn't argue about religion, said the letter-writers he *tells* us in an understandable way.

Thus the viewers. There was a different kind of reaction from his brethren in the ministry. They were hostile, on the whole. One of my dearest friends in the Kirk attacked me for letting loose this "sentimentalist, this wishy-washy liberal". It was ever thus with the successful religious broadcaster. His brethren, who saw themselves as much more able to carry through what he was doing, were ungenerous and derogatory. Call it professional jealousy or what you will, this was one of the hardest facts I had to stomach in my work. At the time I had to decide whether Willie should be asked to do a new series; I put the question to a conference of twenty representative parish ministers. Only one said, "Go ahead!" It took five years of his brilliant communication before parish ministers at last recognised that he was an immense ally to their cause.

The next Barclay series, in 1963, christened "Studio A", the largest TV studio outside London. This time we omitted the students, as requested, and arranged to have a studio audience of some sixty people to whom Willie would speak. Still obsessed with the argumentative, "Meeting Point" approach, the last ten minutes of each lecture were given over to questions from the audience. Our Design people gave us a splendid set, we gathered articulate lay folk from half-a-dozen churches, we flooded them all with lights and manoeuvred cameras in and out amongst them in the best Light Entertainment manner, and hey presto, we had another successful Barclay series.

Reactions were even more lyrical than for Series I. But as previously, the viewers had no time at all for the "sacred cow" of audience-participation. It was Religious Broadcasting heresy, in those days, to allow any man the freedom of the cameras, outside of church services. Questioning was all-important; all speakers must be tested. How dare we thrust any man's opinions down people's throats on matters of belief and unbelief!

But Religious Broadcasting policy, in this respect, was out of step with what was happening elsewhere in television where we had experts dominating the screens, men such as General Sir Brian Horrocks on Military matters, Patrick Moore on Astronomy, A. J. P. Taylor on modern history, Sir Kenneth Clark on a wide variety of cultural matters, etc., etc. Then something happened which opened my eyes to the fallacy of this form of censorship. Willie preached one Sunday in my own parish church, Newlands South. I had never before seen him in public action, despite his many radio broadcasts and TV appearances. I was totally fascinated. There he was, in a smallish pulpit, wholly caught up in his subject. He moved around his rostrum with great vigour; he gesticulated, stabbed his finger at the congregation, turned this way and that, adjusted his hearing-aid, all with complete naturalness. As I watched, it dawned on me that I had been trying to make Barclay conform to the television conventions of setting and questioning. Why not let him loose in his own environment, a lecture-room, and try there to capture him in full flight, by the cameras?

We did precisely that for Series III from Trinity College, Glasgow, and continued to do so for the next few years until

Willie himself said: "We've done enough for now; let's rest for a year or two." Even in that proposal he was unique; no other regular broadcaster ever said: "Enough for now!" Most didn't even know when they had exhausted their particular gifts and resented it deeply when we had to move away from them for reasons clear enough to the viewers and to us, but not to them.

Willie and I prepared thoroughly for each new series. We would meet six months before it began and talk through reactions to the past one and a subject for the next. Willie would then work out his scripts in broad outline. These he would then test on his students and other groups to whom he lectured. He would let me have a rough copy of what he proposed to say, on the understanding that he would deliver it freely in his own way. Meantime we gathered together an audience from men's groups, women's guilds, youth groups and any other gathering Willie had been working with, irrespective of denomination or none. We moved our O.B. Unit into Trinity College and sometimes we would record two lectures per night. Before each one, Willie insisted on a complete run-through, alone, before cameras. This suited our purposes too, for he was not the easiest of subjects to shoot. Occasionally a new idea would occur to him and he would turn to the black-board to illustrate it. The several Greek words for 'sin' which had excited Jerry Girot, he wrote up and expounded. Even Hebrew appeared at times. Thus, despite the entertainment value of his lectures, he never talked down to his audience, and that, without doubt, was part of his secret.

As time went on, reports came to us from churches carrying out parish missions, that the people they visited often said, "I don't go to Kirk, but I never miss 'Songs of Praise' and that Professor Barclay!" Over the years, we had devised many a programme to speak to that mythical character, the non-church-goer, but at the end of the day, it was the uncompromising Christian with the common touch who got across to them. George MacLeod in his Govan days, for example, and Willie Barclay in the Sixties.

My favourite Barclay story concerns his communication with the industrial Scottish working man who is never supposed to go to church — if he is a Protestant, that is. Willie had been invited to address a learned society in Helensburgh, a Clyde Estuary burgh with up-stage attitudes. The society's secretary explained to Willie that they were accustomed to having their lecturers appear in evening dress. On the given date, Willie duly decked himself out and headed for the burgh which claims John Logie Baird, the inventor of television, as a son. In those days, Willie smoked upwards of sixty cigarettes a day, which did him no good at all. As he passed through Dumbarton, another Clydeside burgh in every way different from Helensburgh, he realised he was on his last cigarette. He stopped his car and hurried into the first place which sold them — a working man's pub, sawdust on the floor, the air blue with both smoke and the patois of the shipyards and the football terracing.

When this gleaming, white-fronted apparition entered the bar, there was a sudden silence. He asked for fags and the voice did the trick! He was "yon fella Barclay on the telly" and the pub erupted around him with good-natured banter, and questions galore. All about the Kirk and how unlike Jesus it was; the bonhomie tinged with that friendly aggression which is the hall-mark of the Scottish working-man on his home territory. When Willie was finally able to tear himself away, they lined up, insisted in shaking hands with him, and, as he related in his characteristic way, "Paid for my cigarettes, forbye!"

That sort of scene was by no means unique. It had been re-enacted from university common room to hotel lounge and football ground, all over Scotland. Once on the morning after a Lecture, I sat with him in his own university's common room and was astonished at the number of staff men and women who came over to him and made some comment on the previous night's lecture. He remarked sadly to me that the only faculty in the University which never seemed to notice his programmes was his own! I later had proof of this professional jealousy when first one, then another, of his faculty sought me out to tell me how much better they would be than W. B. and that, in any case, their theology was sounder. One of them actually took me out to dinner in an expensive restaurant. As the evening went on, I was more and more mystified, until at last out came his proposition. Poor man, he hadn't an iota of Willie's charisma and he talked in a language which members of his own university, outside his faculty, would never have understood.

This kind of thing could be rough going at times. A distinguished churchman at one General Assembly laid hold of me at a General Assembly, and roundly declared I was doing harm to the cause of Christ and His Kirk by using Barclay and his heresies, in any shape or form. As if the workers in that Dumbarton pub, or even the university staff-members, would recognise a heresy when they saw one. What they were left with was an impression of truth and goodness.

Truth to tell, the Kirk never realised until too late the potent weapon she had for evangelism in the Barclay broadcasts. He had the ear of the common man whether he was inside or outside the Church. We knew this. We tried to persuade all sorts of churchmen in authority that it was so, but little reaction followed. Put it down to lack of imagination, or the old green-eyed monster, if you like; it was certainly a fact. Yet I still find it wonderful that the same common man, for eight years, sat at the feet of one of the greatest communicators of New Testament truth in this or any other century. He had his millions of viewers.

On my New Zealand trip in 1971, I showed various types of religious broadcasts to mixed seminars of NZBC staff and clergy of all denominations. At the first of these, in Dunedin, the Scottish city, "Songs of Praise", documentary-films, and discussions all came in for forthright Kiwi criticism. Last of all I played them Barclay in full flight in "The Sermon on the Mount". They watched in complete silence. I steeled myself for the outburst as the credit-title rolled through the strains of Mendelssohn's "Hebridean Overture". Our chairman, Terry Bryan, then in charge of southern New Zealand output, exclaimed, "By God, that's the best piece of religious television I've seen — even if I did disagree with nearly everything he said!"

That reaction happened throughout the country. Churchmen and NZBC staff all wanted to see more Barclay. Eventually these pressures resulted in his being seen on New Zealand television with impressive results. When he was retiring, Michael Jackson Campbell, Director of Communications for the Presbyterian Church, sent a Message to be read at Willie's

Public Farewell:

> As far as I know, William Barclay has never visited New
> Zealand. Yet his name is a household word here and his
> form and features well-known throughout the length and
> breadth of New Zealand.

He then went on to say how churchmen had looked sceptically
at the Barclay Lecture I had brought with me. The professionals too thought that "Talking heads were strictly for
hunters". Then someone said, "But he really got through to
me!" When the Lectures were seen in New Zealand, they
touched everybody . . .

> On Monday mornings people talked about them in trains,
> buses and lifts. Young executives with long-haired
> elegance, and mutton-freezing workers with earthy turns
> of phrase, all debated what he had said . . . Many people
> are wondering why it all works; what the appeal of Willie
> Barclay really is. Perhaps in a society which has written
> off preaching, we are hungry for it. Perhaps he talks to us
> with human understanding and with wit and humour. He
> speaks to us because he really believes what he says
> matters and he communicates to us that we matter. For us
> ordinary folk, all this adds up to the fact that he makes his
> faith live and his God real.

Across the Tasman Sea, there was an even more interesting
tale to tell. The Rev. James Peter, Supervisor of Religious
Broadcasts for the Australian Broadcasting Commission, had
contacted me about various matters of mutual interest over
the years. In 1968 after the World Council of Churches
Assembly at Uppsala, he came to Scotland and asked to see
some Scottish Programmes.

Jim was enthusiastic about all the programmes, but puzzled
because he hadn't heard about them through the BBC's
Transcription Department. Now Transcription is the BBC
Department, based inevitably in London, which offers
programmes for sale to the broadcasting systems of the world.
They received our Scottish publicity blurb on "Scotland Only"

programmes, but I doubt if they ever read it. In any case, I suspect they referred religious programme-requests to the Head of Religious Broadcasting's office where anything might happen to a Scottish programme. I tried to by-pass them, but without success, for even Administration in BBC-Scotland always went "through the usual channels". So through transcription Jim had to go. Whatever he said produced results, for he got his Barclay and other Scottish programmes. This is what he said about the Lectures in his message to the Barclay Farewell:

> I do not recall any series of programmes prompting so many letters and other expressions of appreciation. Long after we had shown the last of them, I was (and still am) being told that Barclay's lectures were amongst the best things we had ever put on. From time to time I tried to determine why these programmes made such an impression on so many different kinds of people. *A priori* one would have thought that such a format (a professor lecturing in a class-room) and such a piece of talent (walking up and down, clumsy of build, marked accent) would spell disaster on television. The answer lies in the relevance and truth of what he had to say, along with his patent sincerity.

Jim Peters showed "The Sermon on the Mount" series no less than three times in each Australian State.

Each year I offered the current Barclay series to BBC-London. Each year I heard no more about it. Once, they did put out a single programme of "Prayer". It produced a remarkable correspondence and in Wales they reckoned it had more reaction than any other religious television broadcast.

Jim Peters' persistence had an effect on London. If Aussies and Kiwis understood and admired Barclay, perhaps the English might as well. (One of the arguments used against him was that his accent was so Scottish!) So they put out "The Sermon", but not at 6.15 p.m. on Sundays; much later, after 11 p.m. on Tuesdays. The reactions were exactly the same as in Scotland and the other side of the world. I was fascinated by the post-mortem at a London staff conference. Some, inevitably, had theological difficulties about the content, but for me the gem came when John Lang, then Head of Religious Radio, expressed great delight in Barclay and everything about him. At last they had found someone who could communicate to ordinary people. At last they had — seven years after we had told them of the same discovery.

The next step in the London saga isn't so cheerful. In 1970 Willie was invited by The Baird Trust to give their four-yearly Lectures. After consultations all round, Willie decided upon the subject: "Jesus To-Day. The Christian Ethic in a Permissive Society". London took cold feet about the subject and the man to deliver it. Barclay wasn't an expert on ethics, not quite up with the contemporary thinkers, etc., etc. So he was excluded from the English, Welsh and Irish screens. But, of course, New Zealand and Australia took him in their stride once more.*

It is nevertheless important to record that every word Willie uttered in his Baird Lectures was firmly based upon his deep understanding and knowledge of Scripture. He read through the New Testament and most of the Old afresh to come to a *scriptural* understanding of the Christian ethic, not only in the permissive, sexual field, but in international and industrial spheres as well. The book of the Lectures has had a huge sale all over the world, not least south of the Border.

What was the secret of his phenomenal success as a television communicator? There were several strands to it, some already indicated. First, his preparations were meticulous. He was slow to come to television, but having arrived, he treated it with the respect of the professional.

Next, he was brimful with his subject; so much in love with it that his joy and happiness flooded over, infectiously, to his fireside audience. Everything he said was brilliantly illustrated by stories straight from life. He had, in fact, closely studied the teaching method of his Master and applied it to his own sphere.

Then he had the immense advantage of being a "character", the sort of personality which at once attracts attention, with harsh voice, vivacious manner despite his bulk, full of gestures

---

* See Malcolm Mackay's contribution to this book, Chapter Eleven.

and the ever-present whines of his hearing-aid. Up and down the rostrum he would pound, stopping to emphasise a point with a whirl of the arms, His total being, physical, academic, spiritual, and not least his humanity, was caught up into one unforgettable whole of dynamic communication.

But for me, his ultimate secret was no secret at all to those who read his works, watched his television, or had the privilege of knowing him personally. It was his devotion to the Jesus he sought to show to people. The Christ was explained, magnified, humanised and then glorified by one who loved Him very deeply. We shall not see his like again.

"Exactly the right words for every occasion"

A postscript on broadcasting
by Douglas Aitken

Douglas Aitken, once minister of St. Andrew's, Nairobi, is senior radio religious producer in BBC Scotland and one of those who worked under Ronald Falconer and with Barclay. This is how he sums up the memory of what was a very happy as well as very satisfying relationship for the broadcasters.

The memory of Willie Barclay that remains most clear to me and my colleagues in the broadcast media is his willingness and ability to provide informed comment on matters of faith and life in simple, comprehensible terms within the strictest of time-limits.

He never said "No", though in latter years we had to go to him with portable recorders. And he never failed to find exactly the right words for every occasion.

To give just one example. I wanted a short statement on "Death" for a children's programme. I went to his office at the university, where he asked about the programme, the audience, and what time we had.

Three minutes.

He took a couple of moments to write five or six words on a scrap of paper. He took off his watch and laid it on the desk. "Right," he said.

I started the machine and he began to speak. "There are three things to remember about death . . ."

Exactly two minutes and 57 seconds later he stopped. It is probably the most telling statement on death I have heard. It is also the most perfect example of his incredible ability to communicate clearly and concisely, at a moment's notice, his burning conviction in Christ and His love.

9 – Communicating across the world
by T. B. Honeyman

Tim Honeyman, a Glaswegian who commutes to Edinburgh, is secretary of the Church of Scotland's Publications Committee. Previously he had been publisher of the Saint Andrew Press, the Church publishing house. He has played a key role in the publishing of the Daily Study Bible *and the worldwide circulation of this and other works by William Barclay. He is a church elder.*

Some years ago a religious book publisher colleague, addressing a conference of religious booksellers, described William Barclay as one of the religious booktrade's "ravens in the wilderness". This publisher friend had likened the clamant needs of the religious book trade and the readers of religious books to the wilderness by the brook Cherith to which God had sent Elijah and where the prophet had been fed, morning and evening, by the ravens. The religious book trade's ravens had been the great authors and outstanding books which had appeared from time to time. New editions of the Scriptures like *The New English Bible* and *The Jerusalem Bible*, and authors such as James Moffatt, C. H. Dodd and William Barclay, whose works had sold in vast quantities, had sustained the religious booksellers in their hours of need and ensured their continuing witness.

But these "ravens" had come primarily to relieve the "wilderness" of the British religious book trade. Here they were welcomed and recognised from other writing or appearances on radio or television. Barclay's craggy features and gravel voice were well known wherever he went. He spoke to the "plain man" and the plain man reached out to him for help and guidance in everyday living, based on a sure foundation of belief. What about the demand from overseas, from ministers and priests, teachers and students, rich and poor?

The American demand for books by William Barclay is more easily understood. His fame as an outstanding teacher and fascinating communicator was spread not only by his post-graduate students, mainly from the United States, at Glasgow University, but also by the hundreds of people, ministers and lay persons, men and women, who flocked to attend the annual summer schools of theology held in Scotland (St. Andrews). In Willie Barclay they found not just an excellent teacher but a vital personality who communicated the message of the New Testament in new and lively ways. Here was no stuffy academic descending from his ivory tower of learning to drop a few pearls of incomprehensible wisdom. Here was an academic whose personal endeavour was to open doors of thought and new ideas so that many more than just other academics might pass through them to richer experiences and understanding.

It was little wonder therefore that the American visitors began to clamour for copies of Professor Barclay's writings on the New Testament. And American religious book publishers were not slow to see the advantages to be gained from having a Barclay title on their lists.

Important authors today are almost obliged to make tours, both at home and abroad, to publicise his or her latest bestseller. While this practice may not be so common in relation to religious books, it is by no means unknown in this field also. William Barclay never made a promotional tour in Great Britain, nor did he, apart from a year's study as a young man at Marburg in Germany, ever visit overseas to lecture or preach though he had received, and refused, countless and repeated invitations to do so.

To hear and see a great preacher or teacher expound his beliefs in person may be highly stimulating by reason of the personal magnetism or charisma of the speaker. There are few, however, who can achieve this rapport both with a visible audience before him as well as with an unseen audience of readers of his publications. Such a one was William Barclay.

Barclay's first book was *Ambassador for Christ*. Written as a Bible-class handbook for the Church of Scotland youth committee, and for his own church Bible class to whose young members it is dedicated, it soon became in great demand as a simple story of the first great Christian missionary, Paul. It has been published in the United States, Japan and, quite recently, in Mexico.

One of the chief attractions of this book is the wealth of historical and archaeological detail used to build up an accurate picture of that fascinating little man who stomped about Asia Minor and the borders of the Mediterranean in the most remarkable way. Here Barclay is a storyteller, *par excellence*. But his story is always firmly based on Biblical or other contemporary evidence. For example, he quotes the second-century description of the Apostle in "The Acts of Paul" which ends by saying that "sometimes he had the face of an angel". Barclay took the detail in the description and summed it up in pithy modern Scots-English: "It is not a very flattering picture — a short, sturdy, bandy-legged, bald, shaggy-eyebrowed figure: but that was Paul."

Then, quoting what Paul says to the Galatians about their readiness to pluck out their own eyes and give them to him, he goes on: "This sounds as if there was something wrong with Paul's eyesight. Perhaps he was dimsighted and could not see very well." From that it is a brief and logical step to the reference in Galatians to the "large letters I am writing to you with my own hand". That paints a picture, says Barclay, of Paul bending close over the paper on which he was writing and sending a message in his big sprawling writing because he could not see to write neatly and properly. "Perhaps Paul all his life could not see very well," an obvious cue for a quick reference to Milton and *Paradise Lost*.

Some might say that it is this attention to detail on the part of the author that so attracts the foreign publisher that he is willing to contemplate the high cost of translation and publication to see the book in his own language. Maybe so. But additionally, and possibly more importantly, there is in Barclay's writings the feeling of the importance of the message; the prime intention to communicate the riches of scholarship to the ordinary reader. Barclay spoke, and still speaks to the "plain man" for whom he wrote so many of his best-known books on prayer and basic Christian belief.

It is this "communicating of commitment" permeating so much of his writing that makes Barclay so acceptable as a writer in translation. Dr. Barclay always insisted on an accurate translation of his writing but recognised the need to change idiomatic illustrations into those relevant to the translator's and his readers' own experience. Such changes need not, must not alter or impair the main thrust of the argument or emphasis.

William Barclay's remarkable and outstandingly successful commentary on the New Testament, the *Daily Study Bible*, has achieved worldwide acclaim in its British and American editions. These seventeen volumes of daily study have been used by preachers and teachers in the preparation of sermons and lessons as well as by church members, of all denominations, and students seeking to expand their personal knowledge of the Gospel. One has heard quotations from Barclay in countless sermons through the years. And this particularly so in English-speaking countries overseas where pastors and catechists and others in missionary situations have been able to obtain these books at reduced rates through the generosity of the author and the help of his publishers.

This "Goodwill Scheme" probably did much to stimulate the desire for these and other Barclay writings to be published in indigenous languages. Some of the books have now been published in Japanese, Chinese, Korean, Hindi, Arabic, and portions in a number of African languages. While most of these translations have been undertaken on a non-commercial basis, others into European languages such as German, Spanish and Italian are fully commercial and successful.

There can be no specific, ready answer to the question: "Why should foreign publishers be anxious to translate and publish Barclay's works?" Unless perhaps it is bound up with the realisation that through his writings William Barclay's constant aim was, as he himself often declared in the words of Richard of Chichester's famous prayer, to enable men and women "to know Jesus Christ more clearly, to love him more dearly, and to follow him more nearly".

10 – Barclay: ecumenical teacher of the Church
by Elmer G. Homrighausen

Professor Elmer G. Homrighausen never met William Barclay, whom he admired from afar. An American scholar and minister, Professor Homrighausen is Emeritus Dean of Princeton Theological Seminary, New Jersey, one of the great centres in the U.S.A. both of theological study and the Presbyterian tradition, derived from continental European Reformed origins as well as those in the British Isles. This is a tribute not only to Barclay's world standing but to the power of his personality in print.

I

The influence of William Barclay, late Professor in New Testament and successor to G. H. C. Macgregor of Glasgow University, Scotland, has made its way across the Christian world. While his life was lived, his education was received, his ministry was pursued, his books and articles were written, his preaching and teaching were done, his media messages were delivered for the most part in Scotland, he was the centre and source of a unique ministry among all the Churches and the general public. In the person and work of Willie Barclay, the local had about it a uniquely ecumenical character. His contribution was possibly due to the fact that what he wrote, preached, taught, broadcast, and lectured about was a rare blend of the Biblical, the evangelical, the pastoral, the practical, and the human.

While I never met William Barclay personally, I have come to know him quite well. Once when preaching at Wellington Church (across the road from Glasgow University) for a month during the summer season, we almost met for luncheon through our mutual friend, Professor Murdo Ewen

Macdonald, but due to an unforeseen circumstance the date was cancelled and we did not become personally acquainted even for a short period of time. What I have learned about Willie is due to reports about him from his colleagues and friends, items published concerning his ministry in newspapers and journals, reading his books and articles, and hearing comments made about the use of his writings by ministers and lay people in both the United States of America and in Britain. In my visits to churches and with ministers, and my examination of church school and ministers' libraries, I find the books of Dr Barclay. Even rather sophisticated ministers and professors who pride themselves on studying only the scholarly experts are found to consult Barclay's commentaries for ready but reliable sources! One would have to admit that in terms of circulation the volume of Dr Barclay's publications is large indeed. And his books in paperback are sold not only in religious book stores, but in general outlets and on newsstands, along with those of Agatha Christie and others. This volume is in itself an indication that what he wrote and how he wrote has filled a need for Biblical, evangelical, pastoral, and practical literature.

II

Barclay's popularity, which he admitted might sometimes be guilty of over-simplification, was due to his ability to make Biblical and theological realities clear, interesting, and helpful to his readers. He disclaimed being a technical theologian. In fact, he has some rather penetrating criticisms to make about the professional theologian. "They often write books for other theologians, produce confusion, and call it theology." Barclay admitted that he could not think in abstractions. He thought in "pictures", which no doubt made him so knowledgeable about Biblical realities.

While he knew what the theologians were thinking and how they thought, and no doubt believed that they had their place in the teaching tradition of the Church, he preferred the practical and operational theology of the Scriptures. And it was always his aim in preaching, teaching or writing, to interest people and to move them to think and to act upon the message. He refused to overwhelm his readers and hearers. He did not think that one could be brought into the Christian life by rational theology but rather by way of practical belief. There seems to be no doubt but that his Highland background, his experience as a pastor among people, and his nature as a "natural believer" had much to do with what and how he taught, preached, and wrote.

Barclay writes unashamedly and honestly about his "second-class" mind. I would not accept his evaluation of himself as a scholar. Much depends upon what is meant by "scholar". But he won first-class honours at Glasgow in the classics, an achievement of which he was rightly proud. Further, he knew his Greek and his Hebrew. He knew the world into which Jesus came, and in which he lived, ministered, suffered, and died. And he knew the world into which the risen Lord was released into the lives of men and women of Graeco-Roman times. He knew the classical world in an enviably familiar way. In reading his Biblical expositions the reader gets the impression that Willie knew the New Testament world as he knew his own.

He knew what the theologians were thinking and writing in esoteric terms, filtered it through his spirit and mind and made it plain and relevant to his readers and hearers.

Barclay also had a tenacious memory. He never forgot anything he read, and he had the facility of recall which accounts for the profusion of illustrations to be found in his writings. He had quotations for every occasion. A random perusal of his "spiritual autobiography"* will find on two pages references to Plato, Gregory of Nyssa, Ruskin, Carlyle, Shakespeare, Swinburne, Ibsen, Baron von Hügel, James Moffatt, Sir Henry Arthur James, Jesus, Paul, Thomas Hardy, Euclid, Pythagoras, J. M. Barrie, T. E. Lawrence, Origen, and Burns!

Barclay frankly admitted that he was not an original thinker. Yet there was something quite original about the way in which his mind could grasp the heart of the matter and from the vast reservoir of his memory put it into words that are clear and even imaginative. Barclay had an original mind which was

* *Testament of Faith* (Mowbrays 1975)

nurtured and disciplined through his family heritage, school, and university education, and the pressure of his several ministerial duties. He had an ability to work hard; he knew how to work against deadlines; he had the gift of word-usage; and he had the ability to communicate what he knew and interest people in it. If this is the meaning of a "second-class mind", let's have more of them!

III

Basic to William Barclay's influence was his family heritage and his education in school and university. These forces elicited and shaped the unique person of William Barclay.

His birth and nurture provided a key factor in his spiritual and intellectual formation. Barclay owed a great debt to his father and mother. The former had no advanced education, but he had an excellent library. And he preached in nearby churches, always without a fee. Father and son argued a good deal, sometimes heatedly, but they remained friends. From him Willie learned to love athletic games, including golf, a love that remained throughout life, although a bout of illness later on kept him from participating in strenuous sports.

Barclay refers to his mother as a "saint". She was talented, born into an aristocratic family, and she was kind. She died of a painful cancer which confronted Willie with the enigma of suffering on the part of a good person. It happened just as he was about to enter the ministry. In his grief, his father offered him the truth, "You'll have a new note in your preaching now." The leather sermon case she gave him, Willie took with him to every pulpit for the rest of his life as a remembrance.

From great teachers at Dalziel High School (in the Lanarkshire steel town of Motherwell) he gained a love for Latin and Greek. He learned to love the classics and the English language. He participated in sports. He practically memorised Gilbert and Sullivan's operas. Every year one of the operas was produced by the school. Many of his schoolmates went on to prominent positions in Britain. "There were giants in those days, and it was God's gift to me that, even if only at a distance, I knew them."

With Dorothy Sayers he affirmed that the mental discipline of the classics is the best preparation for any form of study. And the tools of learning are the same in any and every subject. Barclay had developed a "trained mind".

IV

At Trinity College, Glasgow, Barclay was "supremely fortunate" in his teachers. Among them were W. D. Niven, J. E. McFayden, A. B. Macaulay, A. J. Gossip, W. M. Macgregor, and G. H. C. Macgregor. Regarding these teachers, Barclay mentions a scene from Socrates' life, in which the sage asked an old man what he was thankful to God for, to which he replied, "That being such as I am I have had the friends I have had." And Barclay adds, "As I look back that is exactly how I feel." The professors at Trinity College, Glasgow, had that rare combination of deep spirituality, dedicated scholarship, and warm personal interest in their students.

While Barclay was generous in his expression of indebtedness to the people in his parish ministry, to his students, to his wide and responsive circle of clerical and lay friends, he paid the greatest tribute to his wife, Kate. She was not an academic; Willie surmised that she did not read a book that her husband wrote. But she was no weakling as a critic. She kept her husband from pride. She was a full-time homemaker. Her father was a minister, so she knew the life of the parish minister. Barclay confessed that he was most "unsatisfactory" as a husband and a father. And he was astonished that the work of the minister did not destroy more ministers' marriages. As keepers of the vineyard, they are poor at keeping their own vineyards. Barclay doubted the advisability of women in the ministry especially if they want to be wives and mothers as well. But he had no objection to women in the ministry. Yes, Willie admitted that he did not know how Kate put up with him for more than forty years. All he could say was that thanks were inadequate. He confessed that he took Kate for granted. And he hoped that while she might not have read his other books, she would read this statement, made in his "testament": "I want her to know, and I want everyone to know, that without her, life for me would be impossible."

V

William Barclay had a working faith that appealed to his readers. He had an open mind on many matters of faith and he frankly admitted that on some of them he did not know the answers. He also believed that very few things really mattered. He had his difficulties with the Apostles' Creed but was relieved when a friend told him that when he affirmed "I" believe it really meant "we" believe, since the Creed was the Church's credo, and therefore he might affirm the faith of the Church but have some reservations about certain phrases. He was quite tolerant of the faith of others, but he had no patience with the "know-it-all" Fundamentalist. He believed the Christian faith was not unintelligible, nor is it totally dependent upon human reasons. He stood with Anselm who believed in order to understand.

His theology started with God, and he took comfort in the old arguments of design and purpose to point to the existence and character of God. Because he believed in God, he believed in a good and lovely world. It followed that he believed in the love of God, but it was a love that was strong and gallant and not sloppy or sentimental. Because of his faith in the invincible love of God he was a universalist. Eventually the love of God would win all persons to God. And he based his faith on Scriptural passages and especially the ultimate and complete triumph of God. "As I see it, nothing less than a world is enough for the love of God."

But for Barclay, "Jesus is the centre and the soul of the matter." Jesus was not God, but in Jesus we see God at work and we sense the presence of God among us. He is the Logos, the mind or reason of God. His words have ultimate authority. On the Cross he is saying: "This is the extent of my love for you. I will never stop loving you, even though you flog me, and kill me. There is no limit to which God will not go to make you know I love you." Barclay followed Jeremias who wrote, "No-one in the long history of human thought had ever thought of God like that."

And Barclay believed strongly in the resurrection of the body and life after death. He was supported to some extent by rational arguments. But he believed we could set no limits to the grace of God. The ancients feared death, but Christians can only fear the process of dying, the pain, the humiliation, the general messiness of bodily decay. Christians do not wish the resurrection of their bodies in order to continue their earthly life beyond death. There will no doubt be a meeting, a reuniting of love, but also a confrontation with truth.

Barclay believed in prayer as a sense of being with God, a life lived in a ready access to the heavenly Father. But prayer for him was not asking for things. Prayer was not a labour-saving device. It was not an evasion of life's problems but a preparation for action in life. God will not do for us what we can do for ourselves!

As a last bit of his credo, he affirmed his biggest "belief" of all: "I believe in the home; I believe in marriage; I believe in the family."

VI

Besides being an author, Professor Barclay was a pastor, a preacher, and a teacher. He started his ministry as a parish pastor. He found pastoral work difficult and exhausting, yet most satisfying. The responsibilities of the office filled him with terror and agony. But it was in the pastorate that he learned that "before a man can talk to another person about the deep things of life, he must establish a certain human relationship with that person". So he grew close to people. And what he missed most when he left the parish to become a teacher was the fellowship of people in the congregation.

Barclay not only held a high conception of the pastoral side of the ministry; he had a high conception of its preaching responsibility. All though his life he dreaded preaching, because it was an awesome task. The pulpit for him was a terrifying experience, and he believed that when a man no longer approached the pulpit with such a spirit, he should stop preaching.

During his forty-five years of preaching he came to some pertinent conclusions about the task. He writes that technique is of great importance in preaching. It is like the art of cooking. "Let no budding preacher ever despise teaching on *how* to preach." Above all, he should remember that preaching must be *heard*! Preaching must come from a compulsion and conviction of the preacher. It must issue from experience and be Biblically and creedally centred. And it should be part of the teaching ministry. Barclay lashed out at topical preaching, because it has not consistency or continuity. Preaching must be intelligible, relevant and issue from a sincere spirit. To accomplish its purpose, preaching demands a *learning* not necessary a *learned* ministry. The two are not the same.

Barclay found teaching to be a joy. It held none of the terrors of preaching. But one gets the impression that he did not feel comfortable in a strictly academic atmosphere. Teaching students who came from varied and uneven educational backgrounds posed a problem for him. He enjoyed best the teaching of the first-year class in New Testament and we can guess the reason why.

Teaching brought on some nasty criticisms of some of Barclay's Biblical and theological positions. Here he learned "theological hatred" directed against him by ultra right-wing dogmatists. Worst of all, many who criticised him never read one of his books, and never made an effort to know him personally.

Barclay avoided two extremes in his teaching: becoming too detailed, academic, arid, or "painting with too large a brush". And he practised well the task of holding two things in balance: conveying information and stimulating — even compelling — the student to think.

But Barclay believed that his writing and media ministries were the most important things he did. In the parish, one in ten came to church. Teaching in the university was largely to a captive audience. But reaching the masses of people outside, the people with whom he had no effective contact at all, was a challenge. Through his writings Barclay experienced the ecumenical reality. People who read him were from all denominations and no denomination. The circulation of his paperback books amazed and encouraged him. But radio and television were media aimed to reach the man "outside". During a broadcast, his studio director turned to Barclay and said, "There's a man in a house in a room reading the Sunday paper. *Stop him!*" "What a challenge," said Barclay. From this he learned never to underrate his audience, and that nothing less than the best would do. And Barclay never felt lonely in broadcasting; he felt the companionship of friends. "A Church of the air is not an impossible dream."

VII

Behind the unique, varied, and far-reaching ministry of William Barclay was the spirit of the man. That spirit is communicated to the readers of his books. His was a debonair spirit. He possessed a freedom, a belief-fulness, a hopefulness that was winsome.

He was not overawed by ecclesiastical organisations, sacramental piety, theological pedantry, or cultural traditions. He was unconventional and innovative.

His mind was tolerant towards others who disagreed with him, and he was openminded towards new truths. He had about him the independence of the Highlander. Yet, he had great respect for the Bible and the essentials of the Christian tradition. He was disarming in revealing his tendency towards laziness, untidiness, domestic helplessness, procrastination, and avoidance of conflict situations. And he freely lists all his pet gripes.

He admits there are some answers he does not have on matters of faith and life. He had few intimate friends, and shied away from the tendency towards "touching" and "kissing" now so prevalent; yet, he was a warm-hearted and big-hearted man who loved the people of his parish, his students, his teachers, his wife and family, and even those who were members of his unseen media audiences. He felt himself closer to people in the world than to many churchmen.

He had a great zest for life and its comforts. And while he was sorely aware of people in their painful need, he could speak of his own deafness with a kind of humour, saying that it helped him to sleep anywhere and listen only to what he wanted to hear. And that it never kept him from doing what he wanted to do!

What made him such a remarkable communicator of the Gospel? We have already indicated many influences which formed William Barclay. Certainly his Highland heritage and the influence of his father and mother early shaped his life and vocation. Then there was the education he received at Dalziel High School and Glasgow University under great teacher-models. His pastoral activities and pulpit preaching brought him into dimensions of human relations and ministry that forced him into hard study and a fuller stature of life-in-Christ. A lifetime of inquisitive inquiry, theological reflection and personal responsibility motivated him to study the Biblical sources of the Christian faith with a view to gaining clarity of mind and direction of life. New challenges for service opened up for him and he accepted them with interest although he knew it meant hard work. In it all there was the pervading and supporting love of his wife and family and home that encouraged him. But through it all there is the simple but deeply felt faith of William Barclay. When he was sorely criticised for some of his views on the writings of the New Testament, he wrote that what he believed about these literary matters did not "affect that fact that I love Jesus Christ, and that in him I have the utter assurance that God is my heavenly Father and that my sins are forgiven."

In this respect, he stands in the line of the great Scottish Professors of Divinity who, while scholarly experts in their fields, had a warm personal faith which they preached most acceptably in local congregations.

11 – A late and vital friendship
by Malcolm Mackay

Malcolm Mackay (who holds an Edinburgh doctorate) is a Scots-descended Australian who recently came to live in Dumfries-shire. After serving as secretary of what became the Australian Council of Churches he left the active Presbyterian ministry to become a television commentator, Liberal member of the Australian federal Parliament, and Minister for the Navy. William Barclay played an important role in reshaping his life after defeat in the landslide which brought Gough Whitlam to power in Australia, and encouraged his account of these events in the book "More than Coincidence" (Saint Andrew Press). Mackay also reveals something of the thinking which aligned Barclay with the section of the Church inclined to pacifism, though he was readier to state his position and allow his name to appear among supporters of Lord MacLeod of Fuinary (George MacLeod) than to join in polemical and political debate.

I first heard the name William Barclay in 1951, when I was assistant minister of the Corstorphine Old Parish Church in Edinburgh. A young Sunday school teacher had been to a training course in Glasgow and had returned alight with enthusiasm for the way a certain Doctor Barclay had opened the New Testament in a new way and brought it alive for her. This led me, like thousands of others, to the books which were even then beginning to appear in what was to become a stream lasting some thirty years. Books, books, books — Barclay books by the hundreds of thousands.

More than twenty years intervened before I so much as saw Barclay. That was when he gave his memorable lectures on Christian ethics on television. I myself had travelled a long road from those post-war days in Edinburgh.

I had returned from Scotland and post-graduate study to an outback parish in Australia. From a parish covering twelve thousand square miles, and containing more kangaroos than people, I was called to become General Secretary of the Australian Council for the World Council of Churches (later to become the Australian Council of Churches) and from there to be minister of The Scots' Church in Sydney. At the same time I was busy with the newly arrived medium of television, being an arranger and presenter of religious and current affairs programmes.

In 1959 came the invitation to join the professorial board of the newly formed University of New South Wales and to become master of the first residential college within the university. Five years later I resigned to enter the Australian Parliament. It was during this period, while serving as Minister for the Navy, that I found much of my old fascination for Christian Ethics rekindled by the challenging lectures of Dr Barclay. Like millions of others I had seen what I had thought to be dry subjects come alive as he presented them simply and authoritatively.

One of his lectures in particular, dealing with Situation Ethics, raised many burning questions for me. I agreed with a great deal of what Professor Barclay was saying but found his pacifist viewpoint impossible to entertain. Finally I dictated a letter to him but after reading it through the next day decided against mailing it. I felt it was far too presumptuous for a person who had long since been out of the main stream of Christian academic life thus to criticise statements by such an eminent leader of contemporary thought. My personal secretary however had become intrigued by the letter and its arguments and had other ideas. Even after the defeat of the Government, which meant my own electoral defeat and retirement from the House of Representatives, she persisted until eventually we sent the letter off to Glasgow. The contents of that letter were to play an important part in my first meeting with Professor Barclay and it brought some interesting counter-arguments in reply, so let me summarise and quote:

The first matter raised was the general question of the Christian attitude to situation ethics.

I told him I thought some of the illustrations he gave regarding the decision made by people to take what would clearly be wrong actions from the orthodox moral viewpoint were most readily refuted in my opinion — not by references to the circumstances in which the individual is placed at the time, but by the effect of the acceptance of such behaviour on a communal basis or in relation to ultimate ethical objectives of society as a whole. I told him that my own personal conviction about situational ethics was that it is a red herring making its appeal to emotion rather than the intellect and abdicating from the Christian statesmanship which is required of citizens of the Kingdom of God. I went on:

"On a far bigger canvas, however, I have been constrained to write because I have just finished listening to your talk on 'The Christian in the World Today'. It is in this area that I would give a great deal to have the opportunity of a detailed discussion with you, for I feel that for many years now I have been actively engaged in weighing and sifting arguments that were not fully developed in your talk."

I said that as a Minister charged with defence responsibilities, I had to face continually the challenge of the question of a Christian and war, and took him up on his comment that he could not see Jesus pressing a button for a nuclear attack. "But I do not believe you could any more easily see Jesus using a bayonet on a rifle or, for that matter, firing an arrow from a bow with the intent to transfix another man."

Summing up the dilemma I felt, I said: "I have many times been down the road, innumerable times, to the position of asking whether it would not be better simply to submit to world Communism rather than risk the horrors of war — but nothing that I see in the Bible, or that I know of history, convinces me that pacifism or appeasement of this kind ever bears good fruit, but very much to the contrary."

Almost by return mail came a reply from Glasgow. Barclay agreed with my first criticism but vigorously opposed the second. The foundations were being laid for what was to become a vigorous and helpful discussion.

Barclay's letter of June 14, 1973 read, *inter alia*:

I am so glad that in the end you did send your letter to

me. I am grateful for it, especially grateful for what I hope you will forgive me for calling an intelligent and critical approach.

I have no doubt at all that you are right in insisting that all ethical decisions must be taken in the context of the community. After all, it is the simple truth that there is no such thing as an individual. No man lives and dies by himself. It is just the simple fact that Christian freedom must always be read in the context of Christian communal responsibility.

I am, of course, interested in your words about war. I think that there is no doubt that the advent of atomic warfare would produce a new situation. Obviously there is just no comparison between the damage that a man can do with a bow and arrow and the damage he can do with an atomic bomb. It may be logical to argue that, in principle, to kill one man is the same as killing 100,000 men but I just don't believe it. And I think that weapons which can devastate half a country and demolish a city and have genetic consequences which are incalculable have introduced a new situation. One can probably say that to take a revolver and shoot a man is the same, in principle, as to demolish Dresden. It has always seemed to me that the whole wrongness of war comes in its indiscriminate destruction and there is something quite different in defending oneself by killing your actual attacker than by demolishing hundreds of thousands of people who are only remotely involved in the situation.

I really have to say that, much as I detest the beliefs of Communism, I think we have to give it freedom. I am quite sure that Christianity is immortal and nothing will destroy it. But if Christian principles have to be defended by atom bombs, I would have done with Christianity. I would regard it as a total failure.

This may involve suffering but God's way involved a Cross for Jesus. There is no doubt whatever that Jesus could have obliterated his enemies. He didn't and I think that there stands the answer. If love has to sacrifice, the sacrificing has to be made.

At the same time, I am bound to admit that this is no

orthodox Christian doctrine. That Christian doctrine still believes in the doctrine of the just war seems to me an intolerable paradox.

Mark you, I might feel differently if I had been a responsible member of the Government as you have been. I wish we could talk this out.

Meanwhile plans were emerging for me to visit Europe. I wrote to Barclay. This led to an exchange of notes until finally, after I had arrived in Britain, there came a letter making specific arrangements for us to lunch together.

We met in the vestibule of the Staff Club at Glasgow University. I had arrived a little early, not wanting to keep Barclay waiting. I had the advantage of him in that he was already a familiar figure to me whereas I was unknown to him. While sitting in a lounge chair reading a newspaper some minutes before the time of our rendezvous I was delighted to see him, also early, come slowly through the door and hang up his coat and scarf. Something impelled me not to move at once but simply to sit there for a few minutes before introducing myself. There was a steady stream of staff members coming and going and I began to be greatly intrigued by the high percentage who either stopped to shake his hand or exchanged a cheery greeting in passing. I was even more surprised to see how many of them he appeared to know on quite personal terms. He was like a well-liked pastor greeting members of his congregation. For some minutes I sat there watching him as he made his way into the reception lounge and finally sat alone with a pre-dinner drink, obviously waiting for me, so I went across and introduced myself.

There was immediately the most hospitable of welcomes and we were off to a merry conversation. We chatted for a considerable time before hunger drove us upstairs to the dining room. Here Barclay seated me carefully where I had best access to his hearing aid as we continued our talk unabated. Two-and-a-half hours later he said, "That was a fascinating experience. We must arrange another luncheon before you return to Australia, and I will see to it that next time I am free from other engagements" — he was then obliged to leave because of a mid-afternoon appointment. We made an appropriate date and went our separate ways.

When I returned some days later it was with the strong conviction that I ought to share with him many of the most important things that had been stimulating my faith over the past eight or nine months. In particular I felt that I should tell him of "co-incidences" — things which had happened as the result of faith and which, in my eyes, were more properly to be designated miracles than the outcome of mere chance.

As I told him story after story of this kind they were obviously a stimulus and delight to him. After each episode he would chuckle and say, "Now that's *got* to go into a book!" So the idea of writing a connected story began.

On my return to London en route to Australia I felt I should write to him expressing some of the things that had arisen as a result of our meetings. I wrote thanking him and telling him that since our talk I had felt increasingly strongly that I wanted to work on a book in which I would tell, somewhat auto-biographically, the way in which I had come to a new and virile faith, and the great hope I now had for the future.

Back in Australia I began to collect material for the proposed book, but I gradually became immersed in activities within the Church which made this more intermittent than I had hoped. In 1975 I was asked to go to Melbourne to help with a vacancy in The Scots Church in Collins Street, — perhaps our largest Presbyterian Church in Australia, from which the Rev. Gordon Powell had recently resigned. This vacancy proved to last not the expected three to six months but nearer twenty!

In a letter to Professor Barclay at the time I mentioned other plans which were beginning to germinate in my mind, saying that, as well as staying for some time in Scotland, during that visit I would also "explore the idea that we may move over as a family in 1976 for a much longer time".

Barclay's reply proved to be prophetic, as seen in the light of later events, for he replied at once:

> I am very interested in the plans which you outline in the letter. I don't think there should be any difficulty in getting what we call in Scotland an attachment to some

church, where there would be the opportunity to preach and the opportunity to meet people.

It seems to me the best thing of all might be for you to become a locum in a vacancy for a limited amount of time, either in Glasgow or Edinburgh, for living in these cities would keep you in touch with the mainstream of life in Scotland. *(I later spent seven months as locum for the historic St. Michael's Kirk in Dumfries.)*

I should be happy to do anything I can to arrange for this to be done.

By July 21, 1976 I was able to tell him that the die was now cast for our translation to Scotland. During my earlier visit I had stayed with friends in Moniaive who were living in an old farmhouse which had been transformed into a very comfortable home. I now discovered that they were being forced to sell it and wrote to say that we had decided to buy it from them. Barclay replied, "It is a beautiful spot and not too isolated and I should be able to see quite a bit of you when you come to stay there."

A few days after we had finally settled into Moniaive, in January, 1976, a letter arrived from Barclay indicating that he would like me to come up to the city whenever possible to lunch in the College rooms and talk. At the same time he acknowledged receipt of the first two chapters of manuscript for the book which I was now busy writing. By this time our letters were on a Christian-name basis and it was always a great thrill to find a note signed "Willie".

I recall one of those luncheons when I raised the topic of the way I believed we Christians had shrunk the global significance of Jesus of Nazareth to make him just one more of the religious leaders of the world, the patron of the many religious sects of mankind. I put it this way:

It seems to me that when Jesus said "No man comes to the Father but by me", he could be interpreted in two ways. One way would be to argue that, unless a man became a Christian in the technical sense, subscribing to the basic Christian creed, then he could not truly know God. The other way would be to assert that no man can have a true and valid experience of God, whether he yet sees and understands it or not, except through Christ, for Christ is the Word by which the one and only God enters his created world.

Barclay said instantly:

> Of course it is the second, but remember, Jesus did not say "No man can come to GOD but by me", but "No man can come to the FATHER but by me". There is the difference. It is only through Jesus that we can know God as the one whom Jesus could call Father.

During the next two years we had many such meetings, and to my sorrow I saw this gallant old man with his giant library of a brain getting weaker and weaker physically while his mind and spirit were as strong as ever. We talked deeply, and at times he told marvellous stories, for he had a roguish sense of humour. He persistently urged me to complete my writing, counselling against what he felt to be a fatal error of mulling over and over what had been written. He seemed to think that all writers could command the flow of knowledge and skill to plunge straight ahead with their subject as he could.

The last lunch we had together in Glasgow was on my birthday, December 29, 1977. It arose out of an invitation Willie had sent me after reading a great deal more of the book which was now nearing completion.

He wrote: "More than Coincidence seems to me a good title and leaves you scope for the kind of thing you would like to do." He added Christmas and New Year good wishes and went on to make a specific proposal for us to meet for lunch at the Royal Scottish Automobile Club.

When he arrived on that occasion I was most unhappy to see the change in my friend. I knew that he had many serious health problems but it was clear that his health was deteriorating rapidly. We went in to lunch and here he greeted table after table of businessmen who recognised him at once. He was in particularly good spirits and told a number of delightful stories. One story in particular arose out of our discussion of our surroundings in a very well-appointed club.

He began: "Do you know the story about old Lord Birkenhead and the Athenaeum Club?" When I indicated that I did not he regaled me with the tale of how Lord Birkenhead, in his increasing age, found the journey from his home to the House of Lords something of a trial because of his need to find a place to stop en route. It so happened that although he was not a member, the very exclusive Athenaeum Club was conveniently situated, and he began a habit of availing himself of its facilities. Members of the club soon noticed this however and rather resented the use he was making of their institution as a non-member. They spoke to the secretary about it, urging him to confront the old peer at his next visit. The secretary, overcoming his trepidation, began, "Good morning sir, are you a member of this club?" Birkenhead fixed him with a glare and a feigned look of astonishment, and barked out: "Oh! Is this a club as well?"

At this time Professor Barclay had received almost the whole of what was to be the final manuscript of *More than Coincidence*, but I was only to see him once more, and that was when I was invited to have afternoon tea with him in the very early days of January, 1978. Mrs Barclay had prepared a delightful repast and I sat chatting with Willie, who was wearing a dressing gown over his pyjamas, while she brewed the tea. He went across to his desk, still littered with manuscripts and books, and took up the folder in which my own papers were enclosed. He handed it back to me with the words, "I've read your book, it's a real thriller. Do get on and finish it without delay." I was delighted. Then he went on to tell how much he looked forward to seeing it finished.

As I left the house that day I had a premonition that I might have seen him for the last time, as so it proved. I happened to call at the home some days later on the very day that he was to go into hospital. Mrs Barclay met me at the door and told me he was about to leave and that it was not feasible for us to meet at that moment. I went away sorrowfully, knowing that the end of an era had come. A few days later came the news that Willie had died.

In the days that followed there was a tremendous world-wide tribute paid to the life of this man who had poured out so much of his great erudition and faith to stimulate innumerable lives — and innumerable sermons! I know that many people knew him longer and more intimately than I but he certainly had a profound effect on my own life, in fact I believe that without his unhesitating and robust encouragement I would never have dared to uproot my family and come to Scotland to write. Looking back now, my times with Willie Barclay were some of the greatest privileges one encounters in a lifetime.

12 – Reflecting the Light of the World
by R. D. Kernohan

I hope these analyses, narratives, and recollections will not only warm and cheer those who remember Barclay with affection but can reach some of those still discovering him. There is a lot to discover, and even more for him to reveal about the Gospel.

One of his books (already mentioned here several times) the *Testament of Faith*, I first read more than a year after he died. I read half of it on the short flight from Scotland to Belfast, and the other half on the way back. In between I had marvelled at the cheerfulness of Irish Christians who might have been cast down by weight of politics, conflict, history, and sin. As I fastened my seat belt for landing I see I wrote at the back of the book: "Here is a man who explains what I believe better than I can myself." In explaining, he added strength, and brought me closer to other Christians in a difficult and different situation.

He was in his way an evangelist as well as a teacher. He was an apostle for our time, and his work goes on although his race is run.

In editing this book I have met people who set a time limit to his influence — another two years, or ten. They may be right. Or they may be as wrong as those just over 1900 years ago who remembered an even greater Apostle and perhaps wondered audibly if the vogue for these letters to the Christians in Rome, Corinth, and other places would continue for very long once those who were first excited and inspired by them began to die off.

As a subjective test I decided just as this book was due to go to the publishers to read again the first major book Barclay wrote, which happened to be about that earlier Apostle: *Ambassador for Christ*, the account of the life and teaching of Paul which in its original form appeared in 1951, and from which Tim Honeyman quotes so tellingly in this book. I had first read it at a time of personal loss and strain. I re-read it after an extremely agreeable holiday in Paris during a rather disagreeable Channel crossing when Barclay's account of the hazards of classical Mediterranean mariners was just too relevant for comfort. It stood the triple test of the passage of time, of a deliberately critical approach, and of a potentially contagious malaise spread by passengers sailing into visible and audible distress. It left me reasonably certain that Barclay will communicate the good news for a long time to come as an ambassador for Christ in print.

One of the lessons of Christian history is that really great communicators of the faith speak to very different times and places from their own. Augustine appeared the other day in a modern English version of the *Confessions*. Bunyan flourished in our century in the great age of radio and will return again. Seventeenth-century English Puritans forgotten in their homeland still sell in the remote Hebrides. Jakob Boehm and William Law find new publishers in the age temporarily caught up with the Moonies or transcendental meditators.

Who knows where and how the influence of Barclay may still be felt?

But perhaps the last word deserves to go to those who were moved by him and helped by him. The poem which follows is one of several which came to me, without ambition or pretension, when Barclay died, from people I did not know, and whom he possibly did not know very well or even at all, but who found something in his memory too deep for tears.

Doris Campbell, whose poem is printed on the next page is an Open University student. She lives not far from Glasgow University, with which Barclay was so intimately associated.

William Barclay

Hand on ear, rasping voice, ready smile,
Chalk poised,
A plain man ready to unfold
To all plain men the wealth untold
Of God's Word.
The voice is stilled, and yet it lives
In printed page,
In heart of student, housewife, priest,
Their daily round enriched,
Drawn nearer God.

Freed from earth's limits does he now
Talk with those
Of whom he wrote, and some who disagreed?
For scholars never yet saw eye to eye
On every point.
This I know, a great but humble man
Has passed,
Nor would he wish a monument in stone,
But only this — the opened Word
In your hand.

DORIS CAMPBELL

Barclay and his books: a bibliographical appendix
by R. D. Kernohan

More than fifty . . . at least sixty . . . any advance on seventy? If, as is alleged, Willie Barclay himself didn't know exactly how many books he had written, then there is some hope for the rest of us. Because of the astonishing flow of his work it is easy to lose count or miss out something. There is also the problem of different publishers for editions of the same book, quite apart from the number of publishers (at least a dozen in Britain alone) who had a major or minor share in his output. Added to that are variations in title as well as content when books were republished, and even problems of what constitutes a book.

At the time of writing the Church of Scotland bookshops have a stock-list of nearly fifty Barclay titles, apart from the revised edition of the *Daily Study Bible*, which is really seventeen books plus an index volume. But this list also reaches down to a 10p pamphlet, *Thou shalt not kill* from the Fellowship of Reconciliation (1967).

The fullest Barclay bibliography I have encountered is at the end of Clive Rawlins' collection of Barclay reviews *Men and Affairs* (Mowbrays, 1978). There are, of course, the fragmented entries in the standard bibliographical records. But as Rawlins points out in his chapter in this book the list is not complete. It also includes (see below) a William Barclay whose very different work has been confused in one of the standard records with the Glasgow Protestant professor! Rawlins' count comes to between seventy and seventy-five books, according to what one regards as a separate work.

But anyone eager to earn a Ph.D. with an exhaustive bibliographical thesis on Barclay would also have to take account of separate American and Canadian editions, books translated into various European and other languages, regular magazine and occasional newspaper journalism, and the forewords or blessings which Barclay generously bestowed on others breaking into print. There are also the special lectureships listed by Rawlins (not all of which produced books) and the many broadcasts of various kinds. Where tapes or transcripts of these exist they would merit a place in any "collected works".

I began editing this book preferring the cautious formula that Barclay wrote "more than fifty" books. I end it more inclined to suggest "nearly eighty" as a fair summing-up.

The total edges upward if one accepts a point of bibliographical departure provided by Barclay himself in the ninth part of the Church of Scotland's *Fasti*, the records of its ministers' careers. This part ends at 1954, though it was not published till later. It shows his first book to be *New Testament Studies* (Scottish Sunday School Union, 1937) as Rawlins records in this book. But Barclay, in these days before his high tides, listed other early works as well as his editorship of the *Scottish Sunday School Teacher* (1943–47). For good measure he added his authorship of the New Testament Section of the *Syllabus of Religious Education for Scottish Day Schools* which appeared in parts for school years. First Year, 1945; Second Year, 1947; and Third Year, 1949.

In 1950 by the *Fasti* record, or 1951 by the publisher's imprint, came *Ambassador for Christ*, now encountered in the 1974 Saint Andrew Press revised edition, but starting life as a Bible class handbook of the Church of Scotland Youth Committee. In 1950 came also the first of three Boys' Brigade handbooks listed in the *Fasti*, *God's Plan for Man*. Other early B.B. handbooks were *One Lord, One Faith, One Life* (1952), and *God's Law, God's Sovereignty, and God's Man* (1954). There were echoes of these titles in two later B.B. handbooks from which Barclay shaped *God's Young Church* in 1970 (Saint Andrew Press). These were *God's Man, God's Church, and God's Law*, and *God's Law, God's Servants, and God's Men*. Thereafter (since Rawlins has provided a chronological list) the most helpful way to introduce the reader to the range of Barclay's books may be to categorise them.

The first category, a virtual library in itself, is the *Daily Study Bible* (DSB). The volumes on Acts and Luke appeared in 1953, at which time a series of "daily Bible readings" was developing towards a "daily study Bible". The impact of Barclay's volume on Acts changed its direction and it became a New Testament Barclay series. It was completed in 1959 and a revised version of the series appeared in 1975–76. The original Galatians volume had been combined with Ephesians in 1958 and the same pattern was followed in the revised version. In both editions the work was published by the Saint Andrew Press (SAP), the name adopted from 1954 by the Church of Scotland's book publishing. Previously there had been the Publications or Youth Committee imprints found on the earliest Barclay books of the 1950's.

Perhaps the next convenient category is of books about the Man who is the New Testament. But before books about Jesus (other than the DSB) must come the New Testament itself in Barclay's definitive translation, as distinct from the working version scattered through the DSB. It was published by Collins in 1968–69, first the Gospels and Acts, then the Epistles and Revelation. Of course in a sense all Barclay's books are about Jesus, just as all Paul's letters are about Him. *And Jesus Said* (SAP) started life in 1952 as a Bible class handbook on the Parables. The *All-sufficient Christ* is about Colossians (see below). *Crucified and Crowned* (SCM) links the last days of Jesus's ministry with the beginning of the Church. *The Mind of Jesus*, also SCM, came a year later (1962). The third of this SCM group is *Jesus as they saw Him* (1962) about the titles of our Lord.

A New People's Life of Jesus (SCM, 1965) has slightly different titles across the Atlantic. *Jesus of Nazareth* and *Jesus of Nazareth: the Easter Story* (Collins, 1977) are linked to a TV production. A different kind of visual impact comes in *A Life of Christ* (Darton, Longman, and Todd, 1977) in which Barclay wrote the commentary for a strip cartoon Gospel, working with Iain Reid and artist Eric Fraser. He also found his own face interpolated in cartoon form, for example in the Parable of the Sower.

And He had compassion on them (SAP, 1975) is a study of the Miracles in Bible class handbook form. Rawlins lists *Jesus Christ for To-day* (1974) and *The Christian Way* (1962) but not the Collins version (1960) of the American Scripture Gift Book *The Way, the Truth, and the Life* in which Barclay supplied text for pictures by Ralph Pallen Coleman.

A relatively compact category of Barclay books deals with the early Church, and not least Paul's contribution to it, theme of *Ambassador for Christ. The Mind of St. Paul* came from Collins in 1958. *Flesh and Spirit* (SCM, 1962) is a study on Galatians and the *All-sufficient Christ* on Colossians (SCM, 1964). The same category can cover the studies in conversion in *Turning to God* (SCM, 1963); *God's Young Church* (SAP, 1970); the *Letters to Seven Churches* (about Revelation, not the Epistles, SCM, 1957); and *The Master's Men*, about the Apostles (SCM, 1959). *Educational Ideas in the Ancient World* (Collins, 1959) is indirectly related to the same theme, if not part of it. *The Epistle to the Hebrews* belongs to the Bible Guide series (1965).

That series, which Barclay co-edited with F. F. Bruce (1961–69) began with Barclay's *The Making of the Bible* (Lutterworth, 1961) which can also serve as a step into a broader category of Biblical teaching in his books. *Introducing the Bible* is a later book (Denholm House Press, 1972). *Bible and History* (Lutterwoth, 1968) hovers on the edge of the previous category but *The Character of God*

(Denholm House Press, 1977) is a general statement whose title is its own best description.

Biblical teaching is related to Barclay's New Testament specialisation in *The First Three Gospels* (SCM, 1966), which became *The Gospels and Acts* in 1972 when revised and extended. The 1955 *New Testament Wordbook* (SCM) was followed by *More New Testament Words* (1958) and the two became *A New Testament Wordbook* (1964). SAP books in this group include *The King and the Kingdom* on Israel's vision of the Kingdom of God (1969, but a B.B. handbook earlier); *The Old Law and the New Law* (1972); and *The Men, Meaning, and Message of the Books* (1976, but serialised earlier in *Life and Work*). *By What Authority?* (1974, Darton, Longman and Todd; 1978, Hodder and Stoughton) deals with the authority of Jesus, the Old Testament, and the Church.

Collins' *Plain Man* looked at *The Beatitudes* (1963) and *The Apostles' Creed* (1967). But several *Plain Man* books fit into the large and broad category of Barclay's books on devotion and prayer, which belie any suggestion that he was only a "New Testament background" man.

There are *The Plain Man's Book of Prayers* (1959), *More Prayers for the Plain Man*, (1962), and *The Plain Man Looks at the Lord's Prayer* (1964). From Collins also came *Prayers for Young People* and *More Prayers for Young People* (1962 and 1977) and *Prayers for Help and Healing* (1968). Other books on prayers are *Epilogues and Prayers* (SCM, 1963) and *Prayers for the Christian Year* (SCM, 1964). Not listed in bibliographical records but still on public sale is a spiral-bound *Camp Prayers and Services* meant for the Boys' Brigade.

Booksellers also list as devotional books the selected passages in *Every Day with William Barclay* (Hodder and Stoughton, 1973) which followed *Through the Year with William Barclay* (Hodder and Stoughton, 1971). Parts of these are in *Marching Orders* (1973) and *Marching On* (1974) in which Hodder and Stoughton and the Saint Andrew Press were associated.

A small but important Barclay category might be called Christian ethics or applied Christianity. The earliest is probably the published Fellowship and Reconciliation lecture *Christian Discipline in Society Today* (1963). *Ethics in a Permissive Society* (SAP, 1972) comes from the Baird Lectures. A year later came *The Plain Man's Guide to Ethics* (Collins). The last *Life and Work* (1975) series *Religion and Life* did not appear in book form, like the first series *Beginning Again* in 1948.

And inevitably there is a category which has to be given the defeatist title of "miscellaneous", though it ranges from the deeply spiritual to the eminently practical and perhaps establishes the Christian links between them. From Epworth is *Promise of the Spirit* (1960) and from Mowbrays the spiritual autobiography *Testament of Faith* (1975). *The Lord's Supper* is SCM (1967). In 1966 SCM had *Fishers of Men* about Christian preaching and teaching, the later theme of the Laird Lectures *Communicating the Gospel* (Drummond Press, 1968, but now met in an SAP edition). This has also a chapter which started life as a Glasgow University extra-mural lecture, setting out the different ways in which Protestants and Roman Catholics see and interpret Scripture.

Rawlins also lists *Biblical Studies* (Collins, 1976) which, as he rightly says, is not by Barclay but in his honour. But he seems wrong in attributing to our William Barclay the treatise *De Potestate Papae*, a seventeenth-century work reprinted in facsimile in 1973. The original error seems to be in the Whitaker Cumulative Book List which puts it among the works of the modern Barclay. The British National Bibliography distinguishes its author from Willie, as well it might. Those interested in this shadow Barclay should contact the English Recusant Literary Society, whose views on papal power are probably not those held by Willie Barclay.

The miscellaneous category also seems the place for the anthologies of Barclay literary and other journalism *Men and Affairs* (Mowbrays, 1978) and *In the Hands of God* (Collins, 1978, following *Seen in the Passing,* 1966). Rawlins also notes a co-editorship in 1965 of *The New Testament in Historical and Literary Perspective.*

At this point a bibliographical essay-cum-appendix may happily subside. It is certainly fallible and probably still incomplete, even without the additional material mentioned earlier as demanding attention in an exhaustive study. But this note, greatly helped by Tim Honeyman's knowledge of Barclay books at home and abroad, may assist readers and even provide a starting point for scholars.

Yet even while this book was in proof a Barclay series of *Great Themes of the New Testament* appeared (T. and T. Clark). A Collins book of his thoughts on some Psalms was in preparation and there were plans for a book based on Barclay tape-recordings.

Checking back, and looking at the question in the first sentence of this appendix, I find that an incorrigible collector might push the total of Barclay books well beyond eighty, even excluding overseas or translated versions, by including minor and marginal cases. "Nearly eighty" seems to me a fairer summing-up. But measuring the good Barclay did (and is still doing) makes counting the number of his books seem simple in comparison.